WINDOWS® 98
FOR
DUMMIES®

Quick
Reference

WINDOWS® 98
FOR
DUMMIES®

Quick Reference

by Greg Harvey

IDG
BOOKS
WORLDWIDE

IDG Books Worldwide, Inc.
An International Data Group Company

Foster City, CA ✦ Chicago, IL ✦ Indianapolis, IN ✦ New York, NY

Windows® 98 For Dummies® Quick Reference

Published by
IDG Books Worldwide, Inc.
An International Data Group Company
919 E. Hillsdale Blvd.
Suite 400
Foster City, CA 94404
www.idgbooks.com (IDG Books Worldwide Web site)
www.dummies.com (Dummies Press Web site)

Library of Congress Catalog Card No.: 98-84307

ISBN: 0-7645-0254-9

Printed in the United States of America

10 9 8 7 6

1P/SQ/QR/ZZ/IN

Distributed in the United States by IDG Books Worldwide, Inc.

Distributed by Macmillan Canada for Canada; by Transworld Publishers Limited in the United Kingdom; by IDG Norge Books for Norway; by IDG Sweden Books for Sweden; by Woodslane Pty. Ltd. for Australia; by Woodslane (NZ) Ltd. for New Zealand; by Addison Wesley Longman Singapore Pte Ltd. for Singapore, Malaysia, Thailand, Indonesia and Korea; by Norma Comunicaciones S.A. for Colombia; by Intersoft for South Africa; by International Thomson Publishing for Germany, Austria and Switzerland; by Toppan Company Ltd. for Japan; by Distribuidora Cuspide for Argentina; by Livraria Cultura for Brazil; by Ediciencia S.A. for Ecuador; by Ediciones ZETA S.C.R. Ltda. for Peru; by WS Computer Publishing Corporation, Inc., for the Philippines; by Unalis Corporation for Taiwan; by Contemporanea de Ediciones for Venezuela; by Computer Book & Magazine Store for Puerto Rico; by Express Computer Distributors for the Caribbean and West Indies. Authorized Sales Agent: Anthony Rudkin Associates for the Middle East and North Africa.

For general information on IDG Books Worldwide's books in the U.S., please call our Consumer Customer Service department at 800-762-2974. For reseller information, including discounts and premium sales, please call our Reseller Customer Service department at 800-434-3422.

For information on where to purchase IDG Books Worldwide's books outside the U.S., please contact our International Sales department at 650-655-3200 or fax 650-655-3297.

For information on foreign language translations, please contact our Foreign & Subsidiary Rights department at 650-655-3021 or fax 650-655-3281.

For sales inquiries and special prices for bulk quantities, please contact our Sales department at 650-655-3200 or write to the address above.

For information on using IDG Books Worldwide's books in the classroom or for ordering examination copies, please contact our Educational Sales department at 800-434-2086 or fax 317-596-5499.

For press review copies, author interviews, or other publicity information, please contact our Public Relations department at 650-655-3000 or fax 650-655-3299.

For authorization to photocopy items for corporate, personal, or educational use, please contact Copyright Clearance Center, 222 Rosewood Drive, Danvers, MA 01923, or fax 978-750-4470.

is a trademark under exclusive license to IDG Books Worldwide, Inc., from International Data Group, Inc.

About the Author

Greg Harvey, the author of over 50 computer books, has had a long career of teaching business people in the use of IBM PC, Windows, and Macintosh software application programs. From 1983 to 1988, he conducted hands-on computer software training for corporate business users with a variety of training companies (including his own, PC Teach). From 1988 to 1992, he taught university classes in Lotus 1-2-3 and Introduction to Database Management Technology (using dBASE) in the Department of Information Systems at Golden Gate University in San Francisco.

In mid-1993, Greg started a new multimedia publishing venture, mind over media, Inc. As a multimedia developer and computer book author, he hopes to enliven his future online computer books by making them into true interactive learning experiences that will vastly enrich and improve the training of users of all skill levels.

ABOUT IDG BOOKS WORLDWIDE

Welcome to the world of IDG Books Worldwide.

IDG Books Worldwide, Inc., is a subsidiary of International Data Group, the world's largest publisher of computer-related information and the leading global provider of information services on information technology. IDG was founded more than 30 years ago by Patrick J. McGovern and now employs more than 9,000 people worldwide. IDG publishes more than 290 computer publications in over 75 countries. More than 90 million people read one or more IDG publications each month.

Launched in 1990, IDG Books Worldwide is today the #1 publisher of best-selling computer books in the United States. We are proud to have received eight awards from the Computer Press Association in recognition of editorial excellence and three from Computer Currents' First Annual Readers' Choice Awards. Our best-selling ...For Dummies® series has more than 50 million copies in print with translations in 31 languages. IDG Books Worldwide, through a joint venture with IDG's Hi-Tech Beijing, became the first U.S. publisher to publish a computer book in the People's Republic of China. In record time, IDG Books Worldwide has become the first choice for millions of readers around the world who want to learn how to better manage their businesses.

Our mission is simple: Every one of our books is designed to bring extra value and skill-building instructions to the reader. Our books are written by experts who understand and care about our readers. The knowledge base of our editorial staff comes from years of experience in publishing, education, and journalism — experience we use to produce books to carry us into the new millennium. In short, we care about books, so we attract the best people. We devote special attention to details such as audience, interior design, use of icons, and illustrations. And because we use an efficient process of authoring, editing, and desktop publishing our books electronically, we can spend more time ensuring superior content and less time on the technicalities of making books.

You can count on our commitment to deliver high-quality books at competitive prices on topics you want to read about. At IDG Books Worldwide, we continue in the IDG tradition of delivering quality for more than 30 years. You'll find no better book on a subject than one from IDG Books Worldwide.

IDG BOOKS WORLDWIDE

John Kilcullen
Chairman and CEO
IDG Books Worldwide, Inc.

Steven Berkowitz
President and Publisher
IDG Books Worldwide, Inc.

VIII
WINNER
Eighth Annual Computer Press Awards ≥ 1992

IX
WINNER
Ninth Annual Computer Press Awards ≥ 1993

X
WINNER
Tenth Annual Computer Press Awards ≥ 1994

XI
WINNER
Eleventh Annual Computer Press Awards ≥ 1995

IDG is the world's leading IT media, research and exposition company. Founded, in 1964, IDG had 1997 revenues of $2.05 billion and has more than 9,000 employees worldwide. IDG offers the widest range of media options that reach IT buyers in 75 countries representing 95% of worldwide IT spending. IDG's diverse product and services portfolio spans six key areas including print publishing, online publishing, expositions and conferences, market research, education and training, and global marketing services. More than 90 million people read one or more of IDG's 290 magazines and newspapers, including IDG's leading global brands — Computerworld, PC World, Network World, Macworld and the Channel World family of publications. IDG Books Worldwide is one of the fastest-growing computer book publishers in the world, with more than 700 titles in 36 languages. The "...For Dummies®" series alone has more than 50 million copies in print. IDG offers online users the largest network of technology-specific Web sites around the world through IDG.net (http://www.idg.net), which comprises more than 225 targeted Web sites in 55 countries worldwide. International Data Corporation (IDC) is the world's largest provider of information technology data, analysis and consulting, with research centers in over 41 countries and more than 400 research analysts worldwide. IDG World Expo is a leading producer of more than 168 globally branded conferences and expositions in 35 countries including E3 (Electronic Entertainment Expo), Macworld Expo, ComNet, Windows World Expo, ICE (Internet Commerce Expo), Agenda, DEMO, and Spotlight. IDG's training subsidiary, ExecuTrain, is the world's largest computer training company, with more than 230 locations worldwide and 785 training courses. IDG Marketing Services helps industry-leading IT companies build international brand recognition by developing global integrated marketing programs via IDG's print, online and exposition products worldwide. Further information about the company can be found at www.idg.com.   10/8/98

Author's Acknowledgments

Many thanks to Michael Meadhra for helping me with this very special revision of my Windows Quick Reference.

I want to thank the following people at IDG Books Worldwide, Inc., as well, who have worked so hard to make this book a reality:

Ellen Camm for her help in getting all the contract details sorted out.

Diane Steele for making this project possible and supporting me all the way.

Mary Goodwin and Greg Robertson for their inspired editorial assistance.

Jamey Marcum for the tech review and the amazing layout folks in Production.

Last, but never least, I want to acknowledge my indebtedness to Dan Gookin, whose vision, sardonic wit, and (sometimes) good humor produced *DOS For Dummies,* the "Mother" of all *...For Dummies* books. Thanks for the inspiration and the book that made it all possible, Dan.

Greg Harvey

Point Reyes Station, California

Publisher's Acknowledgments

We're proud of this book; please register your comments through our IDG Books Worldwide Online Registration Form located at http://my2cents.dummies.com.

Some of the people who helped bring this book to market include the following:

Acquisitions, Development, and Editorial

Project Editor: Mary Goodwin

Acquisitions Editor: Ellen Camm

Copy Editor: Greg Robertson

Technical Editor: Jamey Marcum

Editorial Manager: Elaine Brush

Editorial Assistant: Paul Kuzmic

Production

Project Coordinator: Karen York

Layout and Graphics: Lou Boudreau, Linda M. Boyer, Maridee V. Ennis, Angela F. Hunckler, Jane E. Martin, Brent Savage, Deirdre Smith, Rashell Smith, Michael A. Sullivan

Proofreaders: Kelli Botta, Vickie Broyles, Michelle Croninger, Rebecca Senninger, Janet M. Withers

Indexer: Steve Rath

General and Administrative

IDG Books Worldwide, Inc.: John Kilcullen, CEO; Steven Berkowitz, President and Publisher

IDG Books Technology Publishing: Brenda McLaughlin, Senior Vice President and Group Publisher

Dummies Technology Press and Dummies Editorial: Diane Graves Steele, Vice President and Associate Publisher; Mary Bednarek, Director of Acquisitions and Product Development; Kristin A. Cocks, Editorial Director

Dummies Trade Press: Kathleen A. Welton, Vice President and Publisher; Kevin Thornton, Acquisitions Manager

IDG Books Production for Dummies Press: Michael R. Britton, Vice President of Production and Creative Services; Cindy L. Phipps, Manager of Project Coordination, Production Proofreading, and Indexing; Kathie S. Schutte, Supervisor of Page Layout; Shelley Lea, Supervisor of Graphics and Design; Debbie J. Gates, Production Systems Specialist; Robert Springer, Supervisor of Proofreading; Debbie Stailey, Special Projects Coordinator; Tony Augsburger, Supervisor of Reprints and Bluelines

Dummies Packaging and Book Design: Robin Seaman, Creative Director; Kavish + Kavish, Cover Design

♦

The publisher would like to give special thanks to Patrick J. McGovern, without whom this book would not have been possible.

♦

Contents at a Glance

Table of Contents

Part II: Getting Involved with the Active Desktop 59

How to Use This Book

Welcome to *Windows 98 For Dummies Quick Reference* — a quick reference that looks at the lighter side of Windows 98 features and tasks. This book not only gives you the lowdown on Windows 98, but it does so in a way that is quick and easy-to-use.

You may have heard of online help. Well, just think of this book as on-side help. Keep it by your side when you're at the computer, and before you try to perform a Windows 98 task that you're the least bit unsure of, look up the task in the appropriate section. Scan the entry, looking for any warnings (those nasty bomb icons). Afterwards, simply follow the steps to guide you through the options.

The Cast of Icons

In your travels through this book, you'll come across the following icons:

A tip to make you a more clever Windows 98 user.

Look out! Something in this task can get you into trouble.

A handy-dandy guide to point you straight to the sections in *Windows 98 For Dummies,* where you can find more examples of how to use this command or perform this task.

Indicates the quickest possible way to accomplish a certain task under normal circumstances.

Shows you the cool new stuff in Windows 98.

How This Book Is Organized

For your convenience, this book is divided into four parts, plus a glossary of the strange and arcane technical terms that you will surely need to know:

- ✦ Part I: Windows 98 Up Close and Personal
- ✦ Part II: Getting Involved with the Active Desktop
- ✦ Part III: Doing Everyday Stuff in Windows 98
- ✦ Part IV: Accessories and Control Panel Settings for Every Appetite
- ✦ Glossary

Each of these sections (except the Glossary) describes the various features and tasks that you may need to use as you journey into the world of Windows 98.

Miscellaneous Information

This book is designed for beginners who have at least some experience with Windows in the 3.0, 3.1, or 95 varieties, but who have never had a gander at all the new stuff in Windows 98. If you are really a greenhorn when it comes to Windows 98, glance over Part I, "Windows 98 Up Close and Personal," and Part III, "Doing Everyday Stuff in Windows 98." If you can't find enough information to help you there, then please get your hands on a copy of Andy Rathbone's excellent *Windows 98 For Dummies* (published by IDG Books Worldwide, Inc.), which is a much more extensive reference and provides a good starting point for discovering Windows 98.

The following are some other bits of information that will help you to navigate your way around this book:

✦ To make it easier for you to go back and forth between the telegraphic information presented in this quick reference and in *Windows 98 For Dummies,* I've cross-referenced some topics to related discussions in that book. (Look for the Cross-Reference icons.)

✦ If I think that it will be helpful for you to refer to another section of this book, I include a *See also* note with the appropriate section listed.

✦ If I mention a term that you aren't familiar with, don't panic. Simply turn to the back of this book and look up the term in the Glossary that I have provided for emergencies such as these.

Part 1

Windows 98 Up Close and Personal

Part I dispenses helpful information for the Windows newbie and seasoned pro alike. If you're just starting out with the Windows operating system, you've come to the right place. Here, you find definitions for basic Windows components such as files, folders, dialog boxes, and, of course, those ever-present windows. If "been there, done that" sums up your current view of Windows 95, check out exciting new features like Web integration with Internet Explorer 4.0, the Active Desktop, and the Windows Update and Tune-Up wizards. These and other major enhancements more than justify your having to wait nearly three years for Windows 98.

In this part . . .

- ✔ **Understanding the Active Desktop**
- ✔ **Using files, folders, and dialog boxes**
- ✔ **Understanding Web integration with Internet Explorer 4.0**
- ✔ **Finding different kinds of things with the Explorer**
- ✔ **Understanding all kinds of menus**
- ✔ **Working with my stuff (My Computer, My Briefcase, and My Documents) on the desktop**
- ✔ **Using the taskbar to perform tasks**
- ✔ **Working with windows (the on-screen type)**

Active Desktop

The Active Desktop is the amazing new set of features that initiates Microsoft's grand plan for building "true" Web integration into the Windows operating environment. The set of Web integration features offered in Windows 98 includes the following:

+ **Complete Internet Explorer 4 integration:** You can now browse the Web from within the Internet Explorer, or you can enter Web addresses into the address bar in the My Computer or Windows Explorer windows (which essentially converts these windows into versions of Internet Explorer 4).

+ **Single browsing experience:** You can have the Windows 98 desktop icons appear and act just like hyperlinks for browsing Web pages — in other words, you single-click instead of double-click to open icons, and you simply point to icons to select them. Likewise, when you browse the folders and files on the local and networked drives of your computer, either in Internet Explorer 4, My Computer, or Windows Explorer, these icons appear and work like Web-page hyperlinks (*see* "Changing the Folder Options for Windows 98" in Part II for details).

+ **Web Page view for folders:** You can create special HTML pages (also known as Web pages) for particular folders on the disk drives (including removable media, such as diskettes and CD-ROMs) that automatically appear whenever you turn on Web view and select the folder's icon in Internet Explorer 4, My Computer, or Windows Explorer. The default Web view automatically reports the size of each subfolder and each file within the folder as you select it. As part of the Web view, you can also assign a graphics file as the wallpaper against which the subfolder and file icons appear (*see* "Creating a Web Page View for a Folder" in Part II for details).

+ **Active Desktop items:** The Internet Explorer 4 in Windows 98 supports special Web pages called *Active Channels.* Channels keep you informed of when updates are made to its pages and, if you desire, automatically downloads the new content to your computer. Active Desktop items are mini-Channel pages that reside directly on the Windows 98 desktop. When you first install Windows 98, a single Active Desktop item called the Internet Explorer Channel Bar (which you use for both subscribing to and opening Active Channels) appears. Then, on your own, you can subscribe to other Active Desktop items and have them added to the desktop (*see* "Adding Active Desktop Items" in Part II for details).

✦ **HTML documents as desktop wallpaper:** In addition to the normal BMP (bitmap) graphics files that you can designate as the desktop wallpaper, you can now indicate GIF and JPEG Web graphics files or HTML documents as the wallpaper for your computer's desktop (***see*** "Customizing the Active Desktop" in Part II for details).

To accommodate the features of the Active Desktop, the Windows 98 desktop now consists of three layers, each of which resides on top of the other:

✦ The top layer contains the Windows 98 desktop icons, including standard shortcuts to items such as My Computer and the Network Neighborhood, as well as custom shortcuts to your favorite programs and folders.

✦ The middle layer contains all displayed Active Desktop items, such as the Internet Explorer Channel Bar, along with other Active Desktop items that you subscribe to.

✦ The bottom layer contains the desktop wallpaper, which can be an HTML document or a BMP, GIF, or JPEG graphics file.

The following figure demonstrates the spatial relationship between these layers. Note how the MSNBC weather map Active Desktop item appears behind the desktop icons in the upper-left corner of the desktop. At the same time, the weather map appears on top of and obscures the Microsoft Windows 98 text that is part of the HTML document being used as the desktop wallpaper.

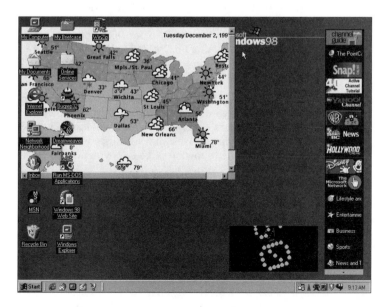

See also Part II for information on hiding and displaying the middle layer with the Active Desktop items and for information on hiding the display of the top layer with the desktop icons and changing the desktop wallpaper on the bottom layer.

Context Menus

See "Menu Management."

Dialog Boxes

A *dialog box* is a special type of window that enables you to specify a bunch of settings at the same time. Dialog boxes appear as the result of selecting certain menu commands or after you open a Control Panel (*see* "Control Panels" in Part IV).

Most dialog boxes appear as a result of selecting a menu command from either a pull-down menu or a context menu. You can always tell when choosing a command will open a dialog box, because the command name is followed by an ellipsis (that's Greek for three dots in a row).

For example, you know that choosing the Options . . . command on the View pull-down menu in a Windows 98 window will open an Options dialog box, because the command appears as Options . . . (with the ellipsis) rather than as Options (no ellipsis).

At the top of each dialog box you find a title bar that contains the name of the dialog box. You can reposition the dialog box on the screen by dragging it by its title bar (and nowhere else). You can't, however, resize a dialog box, which is the major difference between a dialog box and a window — *see* "Windows (The On-Screen Type)" later in this part for details.

Dialog boxes also contain any number of buttons and boxes that you use to make your selections known to Windows 98 or the particular Windows program you have open. The following figures point out the various boxes and buttons you encounter in dialing boxes. The following table tells you how to use the boxes and buttons.

Tabs

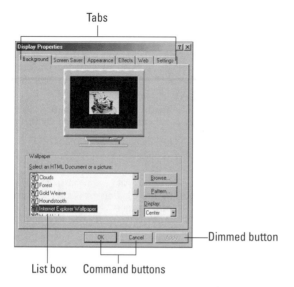

List box   Command buttons   ──Dimmed button

Radio buttons

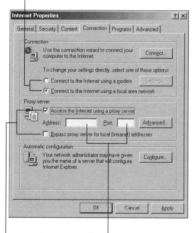

└Check boxes   Text boxes

Parts of a Dialog Box	What You Do with Them
Check box	Used with items that enable you to choose more than one option. Selected options appear with a check mark inside the box, while the current check box option appears with a faint, dotted line around the option name.
Command button	Used to initiate an action, such as putting the options you've selected into effect by clicking the OK button.
Dimmed button	If the command name is dimmed, the button is temporarily out of commission — until you select another prerequisite option.
Drop-down list box	Looks like a text box with a down-arrow button right next door. Click the arrow button to open a list box of possible choices. If there are more choices than will fit in the box, use the scroll bar on the right to display more choices.
List box	Displays an alphabetical list of all choices for an item. Use the scroll bar on the right to display new choices (*see* "Windows (The On-Screen Type)" later in this part for an explanation of scroll bars). The current choice is highlighted in the list.
Radio button	Used with items when you can choose only one of several options. The selected option appears with a dot in the middle of the radio button and a faint, dotted line around the option name.
Slider	Lets you change a value (such as the sound playback volume or mouse speed) by dragging the slider back and forth (usually between Low and High, marked at each end).
Spinner button	Lets you select a new number in an accompanying edit box without having to actually type in that box. Clicking the up-arrow spinner button increases the value by one, and clicking the down-arrow spinner button decreases it by one.
Tab	Lets you select a new page of options in the same dialog box, complete with their own buttons and boxes.
Text (edit) box	Shows you the current setting and enables you to edit it or type in a whole new setting. If the text inside the box is selected, anything you type replaces the highlighted text. You can also delete text by pressing the Delete or Backspace key.

Note that if the name on a command button is followed by an ellipsis (. . .), clicking the button displays another dialog box. However, if the name of a command button is followed by two greater-than symbols (>>), choosing the button expands the current dialog box to display more choices.

After you use these various buttons and boxes to make changes to the current settings controlled by the dialog box, you can close the dialog box and put the new settings into effect by choosing the OK button. If you want to close the dialog box without making *any* changes to the current settings, press the Esc key or click the Close button of the dialog box (the button with the "X" in it, located in the very upper-right corner of the dialog box).

Ever vigilant for alert dialog boxes

An *alert dialog box* is a special type of dialog box that appears whenever Windows 98 can't perform a prescribed task or when you are in a program and about to engage in an activity with possible dire consequences.

The following figure shows a typical alert dialog box — in this case, one initiated by trying to launch Internet Explorer 4 when a modem isn't connected. The alert dialog box basically says "you can't get there from here." Clicking the OK button enables you to start the process over and then successfully complete the operation (assuming that the modem is now plugged in).

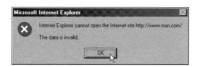

Owning up to properties dialog boxes

A *properties dialog box* appears when you select an object's icon and then choose the Properties command (either from the File pull-down menu or from the object's context menu, which you open by right-clicking its icon).

When you open the properties dialog box for a particular object (such as a program, folder, or file icon), the dialog box gives you information about that object's current settings. The following figure shows the General tab of the System Properties dialog box (in this case, opened by right-clicking the My Computer icon on the desktop and then selecting Properties from its shortcut menu).

System Properties	? X

General | Device Manager | Hardware Profiles | Performance |

System:
  Microsoft Windows 98
  4.10.1691 RC0

Registered to:
  Greg Harvey
  mind over media, Inc.
  24264-XXX-XXXXX-XX-33628

Computer:
  Microsoft
  GenuineIntel
  Pentium(r) II Processor
  Intel MMX(TM) Technology
  64.0MB RAM

OK   Cancel

Most of the time, there's not much you can or want to do with the properties for a particular Windows object. Depending on the object, you may have zero chance of changing any of its settings. In those situations where Windows 98 does let you fool around with the property settings, please be very careful not to screw up your computer by foolishly selecting some incompatible setting that you had no business changing.

That said, here are some safe, cosmetic properties you can fiddle with to your heart's content:

✦ Change the background pattern, choose a new wallpaper for the desktop, or select or change the screen saver for your monitor. *See* "Display Properties" in Part IV to find out how. Remember, thanks to the Active Desktop, you can now use Web pages and graphics for these display elements.

✦ Change when and how the taskbar appears on the desktop, clear all the files listed on the Documents continuation menu, and add or remove shortcuts or folders from the Programs continuation menu. To see how, *see* "Taskbar" later in this part.

For more of what you can do with the Properties dialog box, *see* "Getting the Statistics on a Disk, Folder, or Files" in Part III.

"We're off to see the Wizards . . ."

Wizards are a series of dialog boxes designed specifically to walk you through some sort of setup, such as installing a new printer or creating a new dial-up connection for getting online via your modem.

Many times you will know that you're dealing with a wizard because the title of the initial dialog box says something like

"Accessibility Settings Wizard" or "Add Printer Wizard" and the
like. Other times, the title bar of the initial wizard dialog box
doesn't use the term "Wizard" at all.

Even when the title bar doesn't give you any indication, you can
still tell that you're dealing with a wizard because of the character-
istic Back and Next buttons at the bottom of the dialog boxes.
Also, you can tell when you've reached the wizard's last dialog
box, because this dialog box has a Finish button. As soon as you
click this button, Windows closes the dialog box and puts your
new settings into effect.

Explorer Bars

Explorer bars are a nifty new feature added to the Internet
Explorer 4, My Computer, and Windows Explorer windows. When
you open an Explorer bar in one of these windows, the Explorer
bar splits the window into two panes, one on the left and one on
the right. The Explorer bar appears in the left pane, and the
object or objects that you decide to explore appear in the pane
on the right.

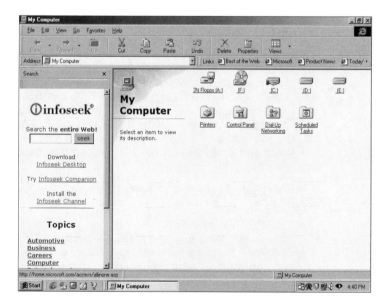

Windows 98 offers several different types of Explorer bars (most of which are Internet related). To display a particular Explorer bar, choose View⇨Explorer Bar on the window's pull-down menu and then select one of the following commands from the submenu that appears:

✦ **Search:** Opens or closes the Search Explorer bar, where you can select one of the available search engines (such as Yahoo!). Use the search engine you choose on the Search Explorer bar to find just those Web sites on the Internet that meet your search criteria (*see* "Searching the Web" in Part II for details).

✦ **Favorites:** Opens or closes the Favorites Explorer bar, which contains a list of hyperlinks to your favorite Web sites, folders, and files. Use the hyperlinks on the Favorites Explorer bar to revisit one of the Web sites on the Internet or to open a favorite local folder or file (*see* "Adding to Your Favorites" in Part II for details on adding stuff).

✦ **History:** Opens or closes the History Explorer bar, which contains a chronological list of hyperlinks to Web sites you've recently visited and the folders and files that you've recently opened. Use the hyperlinks on the History Explorer bar to revisit Web sites on the Internet or to reopen a local folder or file.

✦ **Channels:** Opens or closes the Channel Explorer bar, which contains a list of channel buttons, including one for the Channel Guide, one for each of the channel categories (Lifestyle and Travel, Entertainment, Business, Sports, and News and Technology), along with one of each the channels to which you subscribe. Use the buttons on this Explorer bar to locate and subscribe to new channels or to open channels to which you already subscribe (*see* "Subscribing to Channels" in Part II).

✦ **None:** Closes whatever Explorer bar is currently open in the window.

✦ **All Files:** (Windows Explorer only) Opens or closes the All Files pane in the Windows Explorer. When the All Files pane is open (as it normally is), you can open any of the objects that make up your computer system, such as the folders and files on particular disk drives or the designated home page on the World Wide Web in the pane on the right (*see* "Windows Explorer" later in this part for more information on this window).

In Internet Explorer 4, you can open and close the Search, Favorites, History, and Channel Explorer bars by clicking the appropriate buttons (Search, Favorites, History, and Channels) on the Standard Buttons toolbar. Note that these buttons automatically appear on the Standard Buttons toolbar in the My Computer and Windows Explorer windows when this toolbar is Web-enabled. You can Web-enable the toolbar either by opening the Search, Favorites, History, and Channel Explorer bars with the View⇨Explorer Bar pull-down command or by entering a Web page's Uniform Resource Locator (URL) in the My Computer or Windows Explorer Address bar.

Files

Files contain all the precious data that you create with those sophisticated (and expensive) Windows-based programs. Files occupy a certain amount of space (rated in kilobytes [K], which is Greek for thousands of bytes) on a particular disk, be it your hard drive or a removable floppy disk.

The location of a file (its *pathname*) is identified by the letter of the drive that holds its disk, the folder or subfolders within which it's embedded (*see* "Folders" in this part), and a unique filename. A typical pathname could look like this:

```
C:\Accounts\ISDN\invoice 0215.xls
```

This pathname is shorthand to indicate that a file named "invoice 0215.xls" is located in a folder named "ISDN," which is itself located in a folder called "Accounts," which is, in turn, located on drive C (the hard drive) of your computer.

Let's hear it for long filenames!

Each filename in Windows consists of two parts: a main filename and a file extension. The file extension, which identifies the type of file and what program created it, consists of a maximum of three characters that are automatically assigned by the creating agent or program. Typically, these file extensions are not displayed in the lists of filenames that you see (for information on how to display the file extensions, *see* "Changing the Folder Options" in Part II).

Whereas the creating program normally assigns the file extension, Windows 98 enables you to call the main part of the filename whatever the heck you want, up to a maximum of 255 characters (including spaces!). Keep in mind, however, that all pre-Windows 95 programs, and even some that run on Windows 98, do not support long filenames. These programs allow a maximum of only eight characters, with no spaces.

See also "Renaming Files and Folders" in Part III.

Every file has its icon

In Windows 98, files are assigned special icons along with their filenames. These icons help you quickly identify the type of file when you are browsing the files in your folders in My Computer, Windows Explorer, or Internet Explorer 4. The following table shows some example of these icons:

File Icon	File Type and Program That Opens It
Autoexec	Program file that will install an application on your computer
myfile	Word document that will open in Word for Windows
Book1	Excel workbook that will open in Excel for Windows
Resetlcg	Text file that will open in Notepad utility
ch15body	HTML document that will open in Internet Explorer 4
generic	Unidentified generic file that will open the Open With dialog box, which asks you to identify a program that can open the file

See also "Icons" later in this part for more on the care and feeding of icons.

Typical things to do with files

A few things you will inevitably do with files (in no particular order) are:

✦ Open a file (and, if necessary, the program that created it, if that program is identifiable) by double-clicking or highlighting and then clicking its file icon, depending on the Folder Options settings you specify. (**See** "Changing the Folder Options for Windows 98" in Part II for details on customizing the click settings.)

◆ Print files (via the associated program) by dragging the file icons to a printer in the Printer folders or to a printer shortcut on the desktop.

◆ Move or copy files by dragging their file icons to new folders (*see* "Copying Files and Folders" and "Moving Files and Folders" in Part III for details).

◆ Get rid of files (and free up the space they're taking up) when they are no longer of any use to you by selecting their icons and pressing the Delete key or by dragging their icons to the Recycle Bin (*see* "Deleting Junk" in Part III for details).

As in Windows 95, you can create shortcuts to file locations in Windows 98 to quickly access frequently used files, folders, or Web pages (*see* "Creating Shortcuts" in Part II for details).

Also, keep in mind that you can get lots of good information on a file, such as which program created it, how big it is, when it was created and last revised, and so on, by choosing the Properties command on the file's shortcut menu. For details, *see* "Properties dialog box" earlier in this part, as well as "Getting the Statistics on a Disk, Folder, or Files" in Part III.

You can even make getting this information even easier by creating a Web view for the folder that the file is in. *See* "Creating a Web Page View for a Folder" in Part II for details.

Folders

Folders are the data containers in Windows 98. They can contain files or other folders or a combination of files and folders. Like files, folders occupy a certain amount of space (rated in kilobytes [K], indicating the size of the data files it holds) on a particular disk, be it your hard drive or a removable floppy disk.

The location of a folder (known in Techese as the folder's *directory path*) is identified by the letter of the drive that holds its disk, the other folder or folders within which it's embedded, and a unique name. The following is an example of a Workstuff folder's directory path, which indicates that Workstuff is a subfolder within the My Documents folder on drive C:

```
C:\My Documents\Workstuff
```

You can locate folders on a disk by using these Windows 98 features:

◆ Windows Explorer (*see* "Windows Explorer" in this part)

◆ The My Computer window (*see* "My Computer" in this part)

✦ Internet Explorer 4 (*see* "Browsing Folders on a Local Disk" in Part II)

 ✦ The Find Files feature (*see* "Finding Files and Folders" in Part III)

Windows 98 dramatically alters the way you view and navigate through folders on the desktop. The new Folder Options feature enables you to configure folders with attributes normally found in a Web browser, like Internet Explorer. (*See* "Changing the Folder Options for Windows 98" and "Creating a Web Page View for a Folder" in Part II for details.)

To find out more about the ins and outs of folders in Windows 98, *see also* "Creating New Files and Folders," "Copying Files and Folders," "Moving Files and Folders," and "Deleting Junk," all in Part III.

Icons

Icons are the small pictures identifying the type of object (be it a disk drive, folder, file, or some other such thing) that you're dealing with in Windows 98.

You run into icons everywhere you turn in Windows 98. They're all over the desktop, and the Internet Explorer 4, My Computer, and Windows Explorer windows are lousy with them.

Windows 98 gives you a number of new ways to modify the appearance of the icons as well as to determine the order in which they appear on the desktop or within their window (a job that Windows 98 usually does all by itself). (*See* "Arranging the Icons in a Window" in Part III.) You can also turn off the desktop icons (My Computer, Recycle Bin, and so on). *See* "Display Properties" in Part IV for details.

It takes all types of icons

The icons that you encounter in Windows 98 fall into one of the following types:

 ✦ **Disk icons:** Represent the various drives on your computer or that are currently connected to your computer

 ✦ **File icons:** Represent the different types of documents used by Windows and produced by the programs that you run on your computer

 ✦ **Folder icons:** Represent the various directories that you have on your computer

✦ **Windows component icons:** Represent the various modules that are running on your computer, such as the desktop, My Briefcase, My Computer, Internet Explorer, and the Recycle Bin

✦ **Program icons:** Represent the various executable programs that you have installed on your computer

✦ **Shortcut icons:** Point to files, folders, Windows components, or executable programs that are located elsewhere on the computer

"These icons are made for clicking . . ."

All the icons that you meet in Windows 98 are made for clicking with the mouse — you know, that little white handheld gizmo that came with your computer.

The following table shows the various mouse-click techniques that you employ on the icons you encounter in Windows 98:

Name	*Mouse Action*
Click	Point the mouse pointer at the object and then press and quickly release the primary mouse button. The primary mouse button, whether you are right or left handed, is the one closest to your thumb.
Double-click	Press and release the primary mouse two times in rapid succession.
Right-click	Also known as a secondary mouse click, right-click means to press and release the button that is not designated your primary mouse button. This action often brings up context menus and other goodies.
Drag-and-drop	First, point to an object with the mouse pointer; then click and hold down the primary mouse button as you move the mouse to drag the object to a new position on-screen. Finally, let go of the mouse button to drop the object into its new position. This action is quite useful when rearranging icons or moving files to the Recycle Bin.

Clicking the icons you meet in Windows 98 is your gateway to opening the "object" of the icon. Note that if the icon represents a file or a shortcut to a file and Windows can recognize the program that created it, clicking the icon opens the file and its program simultaneously. If Windows doesn't recognize the file's creator, it opens the Open With dialog box, where you choose a program to try to open the file.

Opening can be just a click away

Traditionally, *graphical user interfaces* (known affectionately as GUIs) like Windows use the following mouse-click scheme to differentiate between selecting and opening the icon:

✦ Single-click the icon to select it (indicated on the screen by highlighting the icon).

✦ Double-click the icon to open its object (*see* "It takes all types of icons" earlier in this section for details on the different types of Windows objects).

Pages on the World Wide Web, however, typically use a slightly different mouse-click scheme to differentiate between selecting and following (the equivalent of opening) hyperlinks, which can be attached to graphics or text on the page:

✦ Move the mouse pointer over the hyperlink to select it (indicated by the mouse pointer changing to the hand icon).

✦ Click (don't double-click) the hyperlink to follow the link. (Normally, following the link means to jump to another section of the page or to open a completely different Web page.)

With the addition of the Active Desktop to Windows 98 (*see* "Active Desktop" at the beginning of this part for details) and its stated goal of marrying the Web to the Windows interface, you now have a choice between selecting and opening Windows icons the normal GUI way (single- and double-click) or the normal Web way (point at and click).

When Windows 98 is first installed on your computer, the traditional GUI single- and double-click scheme is in effect. If you want to switch over and experiment with the Web point-and-click system, you can do so at any time by making a few simple modifications to the Folders Options (*see* "Changing the Folder Options for Windows 98" in Part II for the fine points of putting this new system into effect).

Internet Explorer 4

Internet Explorer 4 is Microsoft's Web browser that is built right into the Windows 98 operating environment. As a Web browser, Internet Explorer lets you connect to and access the information on the Internet, particularly that part of the Net known as the World Wide Web (WWW) — the Web, for short. (The Web is that segment of the Internet that relies exclusively on HTML docu-ments — also known as Web pages — as the means for delivering the Web page content to the user and enabling the user to interact with that content.)

As the latest and greatest version of Microsoft's Web browser, Internet Explorer 4 supports all the following online *and* offline activities:

✦ Browse Web pages on the WWW when connected to the Internet (*see* "Browsing Web Pages" in Part III).

✦ Browse Web page content that you copied to your computer (*downloaded,* in Internet-speak) when you're not connected to the Internet (*see* "Browsing Web pages offline" in Part III).

✦ Browse the contents of local disks that are attached to your computer (*see* "Browsing Folders on a Local Disk" in Part III).

✦ Create subscriptions to regular Web pages as well as to special collections of Web pages, known as channels, so that you are continuously kept informed of when their contents change and, if you want, get the new content automatically downloaded to your computer (*see* "Adding to Favorites" and "Subscribing to Channels" in Part III).

✦ Successfully render the multimedia content on Web pages that use the latest Java and HTML 4 (also known as *dynamic HTML*) technology.

Launching Internet Explorer 4

Microsoft makes it extremely easy to start Internet Explorer 4. You can use any of the following methods to open the program:

✦ Click the Internet Explorer icon on the Windows desktop, or click the Launch Internet Explorer button that appears on the Quick Launch toolbar on the Windows taskbar, to open whatever Web page is designated the home page.

✦ Click one of the channel buttons in the Internet Explorer Channel bar on the Windows desktop to open the home page of the channel that you select.

✦ Click the Internet Explorer logo button that appears at the far right of the menu bar in the My Computer or Windows Explorer window in order to open the Internet Start page on the Microsoft Web site.

✦ Click the Web Help button in the Windows Help window (which you open by clicking the Start button and choosing Help on the Start menu). Next, click the Click Here button in the pane on the right (entitled Windows Update Product Assistance) to open the Windows Update Product Assistance page on the Microsoft Web site.

When opening Internet Explorer 4, keep in mind that normally the first thing that the program wants to do is go online and connect to the Internet.

Regardless of the method you use to open Internet Explorer, you see the window in the following figure.

Address bar · Menu bar · Standard buttons bar · Links bar

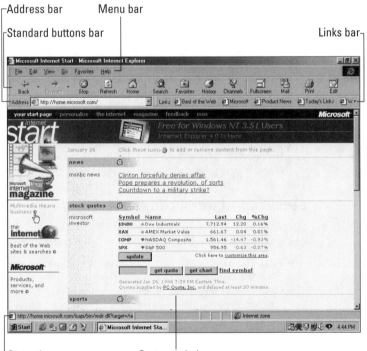

Status bar · Content window

If your computer isn't equipped with a modem (what a concept!) or the modem can't currently make an online connection (meaning you can't connect to a phone jack), when Internet Explorer 4 launches, it opens an alert box saying that a connection with the server could not be established. When you click OK to close this alert box, Internet Explorer opens a local Web page called about:NavigationCanceled.

This Web page contains two hyperlinks: <u>More Information</u> and <u>Helpful Hints</u>. Click the <u>More Information</u> link to display a list of reasons why the local Navigation Canceled Web page opened instead the online Web page you expected to see. Click the <u>Helpful Hints</u> link to display a list of things to try to get the proper online Web page to appear. (These hints are of no help when the problem is that you don't have a modem or you can't connect it to a phone jack.)

Auxiliary Internet programs

Along with Internet Explorer 4, Windows 98 installs some powerful auxiliary Internet programs that enhance its capabilities:

✦ **Outlook Express:** An Internet mail and newsgroup client that you can use to send and read e-mail messages and to read and subscribe to Internet newsgroups (*see* "Sending and Receiving E-Mail with Outlook Express" in Part II for details).

✦ **Microsoft NetMeeting:** An online conferencing program that enables you to make "Internet" phone calls, conduct online video conferences, as well as to share documents and applications on the Internet or the company's intranet (*see* "Communicating with NetMeeting" in Part II for more information).

✦ **Microsoft Chat:** An online chat program that enables you to conduct chat sessions in a chat room, using either a graphical comic-strip format or standard text format (*see* "Conversing via Microsoft Chat" in Part II for details).

✦ **Microsoft NetShow Player:** To play online streaming audio and video broadcasts initiated by hyperlinks on Web pages either on the Internet or on the corporate intranet. (*Streaming* refers to the capability to deliver audio and video content in a continuous stream rather than having to wait until all the content is downloaded to your computer.)

Menu Management

Menus provide the means for Windows to organize and display the command choices you have at any given time, as well as the means for you to indicate your particular command choice.

Windows 98 relies mainly on three types of command menus (each of which is described more fully in the following sections):

✦ Pull-down menus that are attached to the menu bar (or bars) that appears along the top of the window.

✦ Shortcut menus (sometimes known as content menus) that are attached to a particular object, such as the Windows desktop, the Windows taskbar, or the Recycle Bin icon.

✦ Control menus that are attached to the program or document icon that appears in the very upper-left corner of its program or application window.

The following are a few general guidelines that apply when using these types of menus:

✦ If you see a right-facing arrowhead (>) to the right of an option on a menu, another menu containing more options appears when you highlight (or select) that option.

✦ If you see an ellipsis (. . .) at the end of an option in a menu, a dialog box appears when you select that option (*see* "Dialog Boxes" in this part).

✦ If you don't see any kind of symbol next to a menu option, the selected option is carried out immediately.

Tugging on the old pull-down menus

Pull-down menus are the primary means for making your wishes known in Windows 98. (Although most commands on pull-down menus live up to their name and appear below the menu, some (like the Start menu), actually display their options above the menu name when you open them.)

Within windows like My Computer, Windows Explorer, and Internet Explorer 4, the pull-down menus are located on their own menu bar right below the title bar.

There are three methods used to open pull-down menus and select commands:

◆ **Using the mouse:** Point to the pull-down menu (an "embossed" button appears) and then click the menu name on the menu bar to open the menu. Move the mouse pointer through the menu to highlight the desired command and then click to select the menu command.

◆ **Using the Alt key:** Hold down the Alt key as you type the command letter in the menu name (that is, the underlined letter) to open the pull-down menu. Type the command letter of the menu item to select the command.

◆ **Using the F10 function key:** Press the F10 key to activate the menu bar (the File menu name becomes an embossed button). Either type the command letter in the menu name or press the → key to highlight the desired menu and use the ↓ key to open the menu. Press the appropriate arrow key to navigate until the desired menu item is highlighted, and then press the Enter key to select it. Note that after a pull-down menu is open, you can use the ↓ or ← keys to select and open other pull-down menus on the menu bar.

To open the Start menu on the Windows taskbar with the keyboard, press Ctrl+Esc.

Getting acclimated to context menus

Context (also known as *shortcut*) *menus* are pull-down menus that are attached to particular objects in Windows, such as the desktop icons or even the desktop itself. These menus contain commands directly related to the object to which they are attached.

To open a context menu, right-click the object with the mouse.

In the following figure, you see the context menu associated with the hard disk icon in the My Computer window. To open this context menu on the lower right of the hard disk (C:) icon, simply right-click the icon.

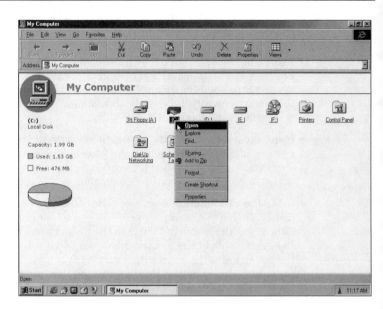

After you open a context menu, you can use any of the pull-down
menu methods described in "Tugging on the old pull-down menus"
to choose its commands.

Context menus attached to program, folder, and file icons on the
desktop or in a window usually contain varying assortments of the
following commands:

+ **Open:** Opens the object.

+ **Create Shortcut:** Creates a shortcut for the selected object
(*see* "Shortcuts" later in this part for details).

+ **Properties:** Gives the lowdown on the selected object (for
details, *see* "Owning up to properties dialog boxes" earlier in
this part).

+ **View:** Changes the size of the icons in a window and the order
in which the window's icons are displayed (*see* "Arranging the
Icons in a Window" in Part III for more on this topic).

+ **Explore:** Opens the selected object and shows its contents in
the Windows Explorer (*see* "Windows Explorer" later in this
chapter for details).

+ **Cut or Copy:** Cuts or copies the object to the Clipboard so
that the object can be moved or copied to another place on
your system or network (*see* "Copying Files and Folders" in
Part III for more on this topic).

✦ **Delete:** Deletes the object by putting it into the Recycle Bin (*see* "Recycle Bin" later in this part for details).

✦ **Rename:** Changes the name of the selected object (*see* "Renaming Files and Folders" in Part III for details).

✦ **Send To:** Sends a copy of the object to an e-mail recipient, a specific floppy drive, My Briefcase (*see* "My Briefcase"), My Documents folder, or creates a shortcut to it on the desktop.

Dominating the Control menu

The Control menu is a standard pull-down menu attached to all the windows that you'll ever open in Windows 98. To open the Control menu, click the little icon to the immediate left of the window's name in the upper-left corner of the window's title bar.

If you double-click this icon instead of single-clicking it, Windows closes the window and quits any application program that happens to be running in it. If you have an unsaved document open in the program whose window you just closed, Windows 98 displays an alert dialog box that gives you a chance to save it before shutting down the shop. *See* "Ever-vigilant for alert dialog boxes."

Almost every Control menu you run into has these same old tired commands on it:

Common Menu Commands	What They Do
Restore	Restores a maximized or minimized window to an in-between size that you can easily change
Move	Moves the window to a new location on the desktop
Size	Enables you to resize the window by moving its left, right, top, or bottom side
Minimize	Shrinks the window all the way down to a button on the taskbar at the bottom of the screen
Maximize	Zooms the window to full size so that it fills up the entire screen
Close (Alt+F4)	Closes the window, thus automatically exiting the program running in it

However convenient the Control menu commands may seem at first blush, Windows 98 offers other, easier sizing and moving alternatives in the form of specialized buttons and mouse techniques. *See* "Windows (The On-Screen Type)" later in this part for more on using these buttons, as well as "Moving and Resizing Windows" in Part III for information on modifying the size and position of windows with the mouse.

My Briefcase

My Briefcase enables you to synchronize versions of files from different computers or disks so that you don't drive yourself crazy trying to figure out which version of the file isn't as up-to-date as the other one.

The My Briefcase icon is right on the desktop, usually below my other stuff, meaning My Computer, My Documents, and the Recycle Bin.

Getting your briefcase ready to go on the road

To use My Briefcase to synchronize versions of a file, follow these steps:

1. Launch the Windows Explorer, open the folder containing the original file or files that are to remain synchronized, and then copy them to My Briefcase.

You can do this copying by opening the folder in the My Computer window and then dragging icons to the My Brief-case icon on the Windows desktop. You can also do this by opening the folder in the Windows Explorer and then dragging the icons to the My Briefcase icon in the All Files pane. (The Briefcase icon appears near the bottom of the All Files pane, right below the Recycle Bin icon.) Note that Windows automatically copies the file or files that you drag to the Briefcase icon as soon as you release the mouse button.

2. Take these copies of the files with you by moving My Briefcase to another diskette or another computer, such as a laptop connected to your desktop computer via a local area network or with the Direct Cable Connection accessory.

The easiest way to accomplish this task is by opening the Windows Explorer, where you open the drive with the disk to which you want to move the Briefcase, and then dragging the My Briefcase icon from the All Files pane to the contents pane on the right.

For more information on copying or moving files, *see* "Copying Files and Folders" in Part III. For information on how to connect a laptop computer directly to your desktop computer, *see* "Direct Cable Connection" in Part IV.

Synchronizing the files in your briefcase

After moving My Briefcase to a diskette or a hard drive on another computer, you can make changes to it as you see fit. To synchronize these updated files against their original versions, you follow these steps:

1. Place the diskette with My Briefcase in the disk drive of the original computer, or connect the laptop computer whose hard drive contains My Briefcase to the original computer.

2. Open My Computer or the Windows Explorer and then move the My Briefcase icon from the diskette or the hard drive of the laptop computer to the desktop of the original computer.

3. Open My Briefcase and, if necessary, choose <u>V</u>iew⊏><u>D</u>etails to display all the file details (including the updating status) for the files shown in the My Briefcase window.

If some of the original files on the desktop computer need updating when compared to those in My Briefcase, the message Needs updating appears in the Status column, as shown in the following figure.

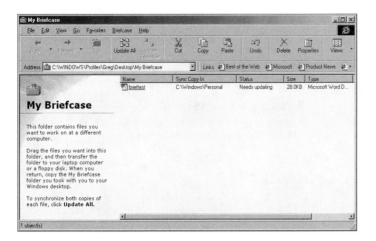

4. To update all files that need updating, click the Update All button on the Standard Buttons toolbar, or choose <u>B</u>riefcase⊏> Update <u>A</u>ll from the pull-down menus. To update only particular files in the list, select their icons and then click the Update Selection button or choose the <u>B</u>riefcase⊏><u>U</u>pdate Selection command on the menu bar.

When you choose Update All or Update Selection, Windows opens the Update My Briefcase dialog box shown in the following figure, which shows which version of each set of files will be replaced.

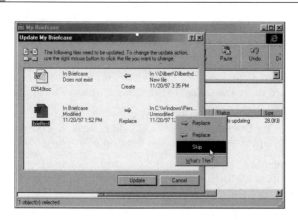

5. (Optional) Normally, Windows replaces the earlier versions of the files shown in the Update My Briefcase dialog box with later versions. To change this order for a particular set of files right-click the file icon in the set that should replace the other then, on the context menu, select the Replace command that has the arrow pointing away from that file toward the version it is to replace.

6. (Optional) To skip any replacing for a particular set of files, choose the Skip command on one of the file's context menus.

7. When you have all the replacements properly figured out, click the Update button at the bottom of the Update My Briefcase dialog box or press Enter.

My Computer

The My Computer window gives you quick access to all the major *local* components of your computer system (*see* "Windows Explorer" later in this part for a window that gives you access to local components, networked components, and the World Wide Web).

To open the My Computer window, you can open the My Computer icon on the Windows 98 desktop, or you can enter My Computer (either by typing it in or by selecting its icon in the attached pop-up menu) in the Address bar (whether on the Windows taskbar, Windows Explorer, or Internet Explorer 4), and then press Enter.

When you first open the My Computer window, it displays all the local drives attached to your computer, along with folders for your printers, Control Panel utilities, Dial-Up Networking connections, and regularly scheduled tasks.

The My Computer window is most useful for getting a quick look-
see at the contents of parts of your computer. To see what's on a
drive or to open one of the folders in the My Computer window,
simply open an icon as follows:

✦ If you open a drive icon, such as 3^1/$_2$ Floppy (A:) or the hard
  drive (C:), Windows opens a new window showing the folders
  and files on that disk.

✦ If you open a floppy drive that doesn't have a diskette in it,
  Windows gives you an error message indicating that the drive
  is not ready. If you meant to put a diskette in the drive, do so
  and then click the Retry button or press Enter.

✦ If the diskette in the floppy drive is not formatted, Windows
  displays an alert box asking you whether you want to format
  the diskette now. To format the diskette, click the Y̲es button
  or press Enter to open the Format dialog box (*see* "Formatting
  a Disk" in Part III).

✦ If you open a CD-ROM drive icon and the drive contains an
  audio CD, Windows opens the CD player and starts playing the
  compact disc (*see* "Playing CDs" in Part III for details). If the
  drive contains a cool game or some other data disk, Windows
  just opens a standard window showing the stuff on the CD-ROM
  (in the case of a game that you've never played, double-click
  the Install icon).

✦ If you open the Control Panel icon, Windows opens the
  Control Panel window with all the familiar Control Panel utility
  icons (*see* "Control Panel" in Part IV).

✦ If you open the Printers icon, Windows opens the Printers
  window, showing all the printers currently installed on your
  system (*see* "Printers Files" in Part III).

✦ If you open the Dial-Up Networking icon, Windows opens the
  Dial-Up Networking window, showing all the dial-up connections that you've created on your system, or the Welcome to
  Dial-Up Networking Wizard if you've never created any dial-up
  connections (*see* "Dial-Up Networking" in Part IV).

✦ If you open the Scheduled Tasks icon, Windows opens the
  Scheduled Tasks window, showing the current status of all
  regularly scheduled tasks that the operating system automatically takes care of (*see* "Tasks right on schedule" in Part IV).

My Documents

The My Documents folder provides a place to store favorite files for easy and quick retrieval.

To open the My Document folder, you either open the My Computer icon on the Windows 98 desktop or you enter My Documents (either by typing it in or by selecting its icon in the attached pop-up menu) in the Address bar (whether on the Windows taskbar, Windows Explorer, or Internet Explorer 4) and press Enter.

![Screenshot of Exploring - My Documents window showing the file listing with 02549pt2, actutor01.htm, actutor02.htm, actutor03.htm, and Xltd97.gif files]

Note that Windows 98 programs such as WordPad and Paint automatically save files to this folder unless you choose another location. To save a file that you create with some other program, such as Word 97 or Excel 97, choose the My Documents folder in the Save In drop-down list box of the Save As dialog box.

To retrieve a file saved in the My Documents folder, open the folder either with the My Documents shortcut on the Windows 98 desktop or in the My Computer, Windows Explorer, or Internet Explorer 4 windows; then open the files icon (either by single- or double-clicking, depending on your folder options). Windows opens the document and, if need be, the program that created it as well.

If you prefer to have Windows 98 open a separate window each time you open a folder or file icon in the My Computer window instead of having Windows replace the contents of the My Computer window with the one you're opening, follow these steps:

1. In the My Computer window, choose View⇨Folder Options to open the Folder Options dialog box.

2. Select the Custom, based on the settings you choose radio button on the General tab of the Folder Options dialog box.

3. Click the Settings button to open the Custom Settings dialog box.

4. In the Custom Settings dialog box, select the Open each folder in its own window radio button in the Browser folders as follows section.

5. Click OK twice, once to close the Custom Settings dialog box and a second time to close the Folder Options dialog box.

Network Neighborhood

The Network Neighborhood gives you an overview of all the workgroups, computers, and shared resources on your Local Area Network (LAN). As a permanent resident on the desktop, whether you're on a LAN or not, you can open it and get a graphic view of the workgroups set up on your network and the resources that are networked together.

The following figure shows the icons in the Network Neighborhood window that represent an entire network and its separate workgroups.

The Network Neighborhood gives you a graphic view of the workgroups set up on your network and the resources that are networked together. When you open the Network Neighborhood window, Windows shows you the icons representing the entire network, as well as each workgroup that you've established.

Keep the following in mind as you work with Network Neighborhood:

+ To see which computers and printers are part of your workgroup, open the workgroup's icon.

+ To see all the workgroups and printers that are networked together — period — open the Entire Network icon.

Online Services

Microsoft has been kind enough to offer easy-access wizards for signing up with some of the largest Internet service providers (ISPs) in the country.

In the Online Services folder (which you open with the Online Services shortcut that appears on the desktop when you install Windows 98), you find icons that enable you to jump right online — assuming you have a modem — and set up an account with any of the following companies:

+ America Online

+ AT&T WorldNet Service

+ CompuServe

+ Prodigy Internet

+ The Microsoft Network (favorite son)

Of course, if you already have a service provider that you're perfectly happy with, just right-click the Online Services folder icon and then choose Delete from its context menu to get rid of this shortcut.

Recycle Bin

The Recycle Bin is the trash can for Windows 98. Like My Computer and Network Neighborhood, it is a permanent resident of the Windows desktop. Anything you delete in Windows goes into the Recycle Bin and stays there until you either retrieve the deleted item or empty the Recycle Bin.

Use the following tips to work efficiently with the Recycle Bin:

✦ **To fill the Recycle Bin:** Select the folders or files you no longer need and drag their icons to the Recycle Bin icon on the desktop and drop them in.

✦ **To rescue stuff from the Recycle Bin:** Open the Recycle Bin and then drag the icons for the files and folders you want to save out of the Recycle Bin and drop them in the desired location. You can also choose File⇨Restore from the Recycle Bin window menu bar.

✦ **To empty the Recycle Bin:** Open the Recycle Bin and choose File⇨Empty Recycle Bin from the Recycle Bin window menu bar. You can also empty it by right-clicking the Recycle Bin icon and choosing Empty Recycle Bin from the icon's context menu.

Keep in mind that choosing the Empty Recycle Bin command immediately blows away everything in the Recycle Bin dialog box. Don't ever empty the Recycle Bin until you examine its contents and are absolutely sure that you'll never need to use any of those items ever again.

For more information on using the Recycle Bin, *see* "Deleting Junk" in Part III.

Shortcuts

Shortcuts make it possible to open an object, such as a favorite document, folder, program, or Web page, directly from the desktop of the computer — even when you have absolutely no idea how deep the object is buried on your computer or where it may be in cyberspace. The following list gives the basic lowdown on shortcuts:

✦ Shortcuts can be located anywhere on your computer, but keep them right out in the open on the desktop so that you can get right at them.

✦ When you create a shortcut for an object, Windows creates an icon for it with a name like "Shortcut to such and such." You can rename the shortcut to whatever name suits you, just as you can rename any file or folder in Windows (*see* "Renaming Files and Folders" in Part III).

Windows Explorer

✦ You can always tell a shortcut icon from the regular icon because the shortcut icon contains a little box with a curved arrow pointing up to the right, like the Explorer shortcut shown here.

✦ Shortcuts function just like their icon counterparts. They open the same way, and in the case of Printer shortcuts, you can drag a file to a Printer shortcut to print on the associated printer.

To create a shortcut for a folder, file, or other type of local object on the Windows 98 desktop, follow these steps:

1. Select the icon for the object for which you want to create a shortcut.

2. Choose File⇨Create Shortcut or choose Create Shortcut from the object's shortcut menu.

3. If Windows displays the error message Unable to create a shortcut here. Do you want the shortcut placed on the desktop?, choose Yes. If Windows doesn't give you this error message, it places the new shortcut in the currently open window. If you want the shortcut on the desktop, where you have constant access to it, drag the shortcut's icon to any place on the desktop and release the mouse button.

You mess up a shortcut if you move the object to which it refers to a new place on your computer, because Windows still looks for it (unsuccessfully) in the old location. If you do mess up a shortcut by moving the object it refers to, you have to trash the shortcut and then re-create it or move the original file back to its location.

To create a shortcut to a Web page, follow these two simple steps instead:

1. Open the Web page for which you want to make the shortcut in Internet Explorer 4 (*see* "Browsing Web Pages" in Part II for details).

2. Choose File⇨Send⇨Shortcut To Desktop on the Internet Explorer 4 pull-down menus.

Taskbar

The taskbar forms the base of the Windows 98 desktop. Running along the bottom the complete width of the screen, the taskbar is divided into three sections: the Start button with the accompanying Start pop-up menu at the far left; buttons for open toolbars and windows in the center area; and, at the far right, the status area with icons showing the current status of computer components and programs and processes that are running in the background.

Start menu

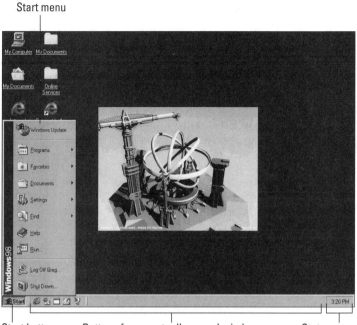

Start button   Buttons for open toolbars and windows   Status area

When you open a window or program on the Windows desktop, Windows adds a button representing that window or program to the center section of the taskbar.

Clicking one of the window or program buttons brings its window, which is temporarily hidden behind others, to the very front, so you can use the taskbar buttons to quickly switch between the programs you're running in the open windows.

 Hold down the Alt key as you press the Tab key to open a dialog box that enables you to cycle through icons for all the open windows on the desktop. After you select the icon for the window you want to bring up front (indicated by a blue box around the icon), just release the Alt and Tab keys.

Taskbar toolbars for every taste

A new feature in Windows 98 enables you to add various toolbars, such as the Address, Quick Launch, and Desktop toolbars, to the center section of the taskbar. You can then use their buttons to accomplish routine tasks in Windows. *See* "Toolbars" later in this part for details on displaying and using these different toolbars.

Status, anyone?

The status area contains icons that indicate the current status of various physical components, such as PCMCIA cards inserted into a laptop computer or a printer attached to a desktop computer, as well as the status of various programs or processes that run in the background, such as a virus-scanning program or the video display settings you're using.

To identify an icon that appears in the status area, position the mouse pointer over it until its ToolTip appears. To change the status of an icon, right-click it to display its pop-up menu, and then click the appropriate menu option. For example, when running the Task Scheduler utility (**see** "System Tools" in Part IV), you can either pause it or open the Task Scheduler window by right-clicking its icon in the status area of the taskbar.

Starting off with the Start menu

The Start button that opens the Start menu (**see** "Launching Programs" in Part III) always appears as the first button on the taskbar. The Start menu is the most basic pull-down menu in Windows 98, containing almost all the commands you'll ever need to use.

To open the Start menu, simply click the Start button in the lower-left corner of the taskbar or press Ctrl+Esc.

The following table lists the commands you encounter on the Start menu (running from bottom to top). To select a command on the Start menu, just navigate to it with the mouse pointer and click.

Command	What It Does
Sh<u>u</u>t Down	Opens the Shut Down Windows dialog box, where you can either shut off the computer, restart the computer, restart the computer in MS-DOS mode, or put the computer on Standby, a kind of "sleep" mode that consumes less power if you leave your computer on for extended periods of time. *See* "Shutting Down Windows 98" in Part III.
<u>L</u>og Off	On a Local Area Network (LAN), enables you to log off the current user so that you can then log on as yourself.
<u>R</u>un	Opens the Run dialog box, where you enter the pathname of the file, folder, program, or Internet resource that you want Windows to locate and open (*see* "Starting Programs" in Part III).
<u>H</u>elp	Opens Windows Help, an online help database that also includes Web elements, so you can jump to the Internet for even more help (*see* "Getting Help" in Part III).
<u>F</u>ind	Opens a submenu with the following options: <u>F</u>iles or Folders, to find particular files on local or networked disk drives; <u>C</u>omputer, to find a particular computer on your network; On the <u>I</u>nternet, to find a Web site on the Internet; On the Microsoft Network, to search for something or someone on the Microsoft Network (available only if you subscribe to MSN); or <u>P</u>eople, to find a particular person or business in one of the online directories. *See* "Searching the Web" in Part II for more on finding Web pages and people with the online directories, and *see* "Finding Files and Folders" in Part III for more on searching for files.
<u>S</u>ettings	Opens a submenu with the following options: <u>C</u>ontrol Panel, to open the Control Panel window (*see* "Control Panel" in Part IV); Printers, to open the Printers window (*see* "Printing a file" in Part III); Taskbar & Start Menu, to open the Taskbar Properties dialog box, where you can modify the appearance of the Start menu and the taskbar (*see* "Customizing the taskbar," which follows); <u>F</u>olders & Icons, to open the Folder Option dialog box (*see* "Changing Folder Options for Windows 98" in Part II); <u>A</u>ctive Desktop, for activating, customizing, and updating the Active Desktop (*see* "Active Desktop" earlier in this part); and finally, Windows Update, to connect to a page on the Microsoft Web site, where you can download updates to Windows 98 (*see* "Tuning up the old system" in Part IV for details).
<u>D</u>ocuments	Opens a submenu containing shortcuts to all your most recently opened files. You can purge this list from time to time by using the Taskbar Properties dialog box (*see* "Customizing the taskbar," which follows).
F<u>a</u>vorites	Enables you to access the items designated as your favorite files, folders, Web channels, or Web pages (*see* "Adding to Your Favorites" in Part II for details).

(continued)

Command	What It Does
Programs	Opens a submenu containing all the programs installed on your computer at the time you installed Windows 98, including the Windows Accessories (*see* Part IV) and Windows Explorer (*see* "Windows Explorer" later in this part). You can control which programs appear on the Programs continuation menu by adding folders to or removing folders from the Programs folder. For more on customizing the taskbar, *see* "Customizing the taskbar" that follows.
Windows Update	Connects you to the Microsoft Web site, which then checks your computer system to see if your version of Windows 98 needs updating, and, if you allow, automatically downloads and installs the new updated components (*see* "Tuning up the old system" in Part IV for details).
Open Office Document	If you have Microsoft Office installed on your computer (and who doesn't?), you can use this command to display the Open Office Document dialog box, where you can search the particular Office document (Word, Excel, PowerPoint, or Access) you want to open.
New Office Document	If you have Microsoft Office installed on your computer, you can use this command to open a new Office document using one of many different types of templates available (Word, Web page, Excel, PowerPoint, Binder, or Access).

Customizing the taskbar

The Taskbar Properties dialog box, which you see in the following figure, enables you to customize the settings for the taskbar and the Start menu. To open this dialog box, you can either click the Start button and choose Settings⇨Taskbar & Start Menu, or you can click any open area (with no buttons) of the taskbar and choose Properties on the taskbar shortcut menu.

The check boxes on the Taskbar Options tab of the Taskbar
Properties dialog box do the following:

Taskbar Option	What It Does
Always on Top	Keeps the taskbar visible, no matter what window or dialog box you open. Deselect this option if you don't want the taskbar to be visible in programs like Word and Excel, even when you run them in full-size windows.
Auto Hide	Hides the taskbar until you roll the mouse pointer somewhere over its position. This way, the taskbar appears only when you need it.
Show Small Icons in Start Menu	Places smaller icons for items on the Start menu.
Show Clock	When this box contains a check mark, Windows displays the current time in the Status area at the far-right end of the taskbar.

The Start Menu Programs tab of the Taskbar Properties dialog box,
shown in the following figure, enables you to customize the Start
menu by choosing what shortcuts appear on it.

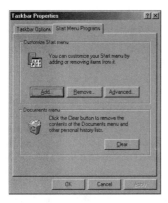

The command buttons on the Start Menu Programs tab of the
Taskbar Properties dialog box do the following:

Start Menu Program	What It Does
Add	Opens the Create Shortcut dialog box, where you can specify the pathname of the program's executable file that you want to add to the Programs submenu. If you don't know the pathname, click the Browse button and select the icon for the program file after locating it in the Browse dialog box.

(continued)

Start Menu Program	What It Does
Remove	Opens the Remove Shortcuts/Folders dialog box with a list of all the files on the Programs submenu. To remove a file, select its icon and then click the Remove button.
Advanced	Opens an Exploring – Start Menu window showing the Start Menu and Programs folders. You can then add items to and delete items from the Programs submenu by dragging their icons in or out of the Programs folder.
Clear	Empties the Documents submenu of all file shortcuts so that Windows can start building a new list of shortcuts.

TIP

You can drag and drop items from submenus to the top of the Start menu (above the separator that appears right above the Programs command). For example, to move the Windows Explorer shortcut from the Programs folder to the top section of the Start menu (where it is easier and quicker to select), drag the Windows Explorer shortcut from the Programs folder to the place at the top of the Start menu (indicated by a heavy black horizontal I-beam), and then release the mouse button.

Toolbars

Toolbars (often shortened to *bars*) contain the buttons and menus that you use to get things done. Different types of toolbars (each with its own group of buttons) can appear within the various windows, such as My Computer, Windows Explorer, and Internet Explorer 4, as well as on the taskbar on the Windows 98 desktop.

When you first display toolbars in a window, they appear docked one on top of the other in neat little rows at the top of the window. When you first display toolbars on the taskbar, they appear one after the other on the taskbar, often scrunching up the buttons representing the various windows open on the desktop, and with spinner buttons for displaying new groups of buttons.

To display a certain type of toolbar in a window like My Computer, Windows Explorer, or Internet Explorer 4, choose View➪Toolbars and then select one of the following commands on the cascading menu that appears:

✦ **Standard Buttons:** Displays or hides the Standard Buttons toolbar. The particular buttons that appear on this toolbar depend on whether you are browsing local files and folders or Web pages on the Internet or the corporate intranet.

◆ **Address:** Displays or hides the Address bar. The Address bar contains a text box in which you can enter the URL of the Web page you want to visit or the pathname of the folders you want to browse.

◆ **Links:** Displays or hides the Links bar. The Links bar contains buttons with links to favorite Web pages.

◆ **Text Labels:** Displays or hides text labels under the icons on the Standard Buttons bar. Note that if you choose not to display the text labels, ToolTips appear when you roll over the Standard Buttons bar with the mouse pointer.

To display a certain type of toolbar on the Windows 98 taskbar, right-click the taskbar (making sure that you don't click the Start button or any of the other buttons that currently appear on the taskbar), select Toolbars on the context menu, and choose one of the following commands on the cascading menu that appears:

◆ **Address:** Displays or hides the Address bar. The address bar contains a text box in which you can enter the URL of the Web page you want to visit or the pathname of the folders you want to browse.

◆ **Links:** Displays or hides the Links bar. The Links bar contains buttons with links to favorite Web pages.

◆ **Desktop:** Hides or displays the Desktop toolbar. The Desktop toolbar contains buttons for all the icons you have on your desktop.

◆ **Quick Launch:** Displays or hides the Quick Launch toolbar. The Quick Launch toolbar contains buttons for launching Internet Explorer 4, Outlook Express, or the Television tuner (if you install this part of Windows 98), along with a button for viewing channels and minimizing all open windows to show only the Windows 98 desktop.

◆ **New Toolbar:** Opens the New Toolbar dialog box, where you can make the items in a particular folder into buttons on a new custom toolbar.

If the taskbar is already full of buttons and you don't have much leeway for opening the taskbar context menu with the Toolbars command, you can always right-click somewhere on the time in the status area of the taskbar to do so. Right-clicking the current time in the status area always brings up the context menu for the taskbar, whereas right-clicking a button that appears on the taskbar or an icon in the status area opens a context menu for just that button or icon.

See also "Explorer Bars" earlier in this part for information about this new type of vertical toolbar that you can display within the My Computer, Windows Explorer, and Internet Explorer 4 windows.

Taking advantage of the Address bar

You can use the Address bar to search or browse Web pages on the Internet or your corporate intranet or to browse folders and files on local or networked disk drives. Just click the Address bar to insert the cursor into its text, type in the URL of the Web page or the pathname of the folder you want to browse, and then press the Enter key.

If you add the Address bar to the Windows 98 taskbar and then use it to browse a local drive or folder or Web page on the Internet, the folders and files appear in a full-screen version of the My Computer window, and the Web pages appear in a full-screen version of Internet Explorer 4.

If you use the Address bar in the My Computer, Windows Explorer, or Internet Explorer 4 window (where the Address bar is automatically displayed) to browse local drives or folders or Internet Web pages, the folders, files, or Web pages appear in the particular window in whatever size it currently assumes.

The following figure shows the contents of a C: drive in a full-screen version of the My Computer window opened from the Address bar on the Windows 98 taskbar.

See also "Browsing Folders and Files," "Browsing Web Pages," and "Searching the Web" in Part III for more information on using the Address bar.

Dealing with the Desktop toolbar

The Desktop toolbar contains buttons for all the icons that appear on the Windows 98 desktop. These buttons include ones for the standard Desktop icons, such as My Computer, Internet Explorer 4, and Recycle Bin, as well as those for the program, folder, and file shortcuts that you create (*see* "Shortcuts" in this part for more information on shortcuts).

By displaying the Desktop toolbar (either docked on the Windows 98 taskbar or located on its own elsewhere on the desktop), you retain access to the desktop icons even when you remove their display from the desktop. This gives you more room for displaying the Active Desktop items to which you subscribe. (*See* "Activating/Deactivating the Active Desktop" in Part II for details on hiding the display of the desktop icons when the Web view of the Active Desktop is turned on.)

Latching onto the Links toolbar

The buttons on the Links toolbar (more often than not called simply the *Links bar*) are hyperlinks that open favorite Web pages. When you first start using Windows 98, the Links bar contains only buttons with links to Web pages on the Microsoft Web site. These buttons include Best of the Web, Microsoft, Product News, Today's Links, and Web Gallery, as you can see in the following figure.

| Start | Links | Best of the Web | Microsoft | Product News | 5:01 PM |

You can, if you want, add to the Links toolbar custom buttons that open your favorite Web pages or preferred folders and files that reside on your desktop. To add a button with a link to a preferred Web page, folder, or file, you simply drag its icon to the place on the Links bar where you want it to appear (this icon appears on the Address bar in front of the Web page URL or folder or file pathname). You can tell where the new button will appear, because a dark I-beam appears at the place where the button will be inserted when you release the mouse button.

To delete a button that you no longer want on the Links bar, right-click the button and then choose the Delete command on the button's shortcut menu.

Messing around with the menu bar

The menu bar in Windows 98 modules (such as My Computer, Windows Explorer, and Internet Explorer 4) contain the pull-down menus that you use to perform all kinds of routine tasks. All three windows contain the following menus:

✦ **File:** Does file-type stuff, such as renaming or deleting files and folders or creating shortcuts to them.

✦ **Edit**: Does editing-type stuff, such as cutting, copying, or pasting files or folders.

✦ **View:** Does show-and-tell stuff, such as displaying or hiding particular toolbars or parts of the window and changing the way file and folder icons appear in their windows.

✦ **Go:** Does navigation-type stuff, such as going forward and backward through the folders or Web pages you just viewed, or going to Internet Explorer's home page.

✦ **Favorites:** Add to, open, or organize the folders, files, Web pages, and Web channels that you bookmark or subscribe to.

✦ **Help:** Consult particular help topics that direct you in how to use Windows 98.

In addition to these six common menus, Windows Explorer also contains a seventh menu, called Tools, that you can use to search for files and folders on your computer (*see* "Searching for Files and Folders" in Part III) or to connect to networked drives.

See also "Tugging on the old pull-down menus" earlier in this part for details on using the pull-down menus found on the Windows menu bars.

Calling on the Quick Launch toolbar

The Quick Launch toolbar adds a group of buttons to the Windows taskbar that you can use to start commonly used modules to get back to the desktop. These buttons include:

✦ **Launch Internet Explorer Browser:** Starts Internet Explorer 4 for browsing Web pages.

✦ **Launch Outlook Express:** Starts Outlook Express for sending and receiving e-mail and messages from the newsgroups to which you have subscribed.

✦ **Launch TV Viewer:** Starts the Microsoft TV channel guide for getting the latest information on the current TV programming in your local area. Note that this button appears on the Quick Launch toolbar *only* if your computer is equipped with a TV tuner card *and* you have installed the Microsoft guide software.

✦ **Show Desktop:** Minimizes all open windows in order to obtain immediate access to the Windows Desktop and all the Windows icons and Active Desktop items it contains.

✦ **View Channels:** Starts the Active Channel viewer (a full-screen version of Internet Explorer 4) for subscribing to, updating, and browsing particular Web channels.

In addition to these standard buttons, you can add your own custom buttons to the Quick Launch toolbar by dragging the shortcuts to your favorite program or its executable file from the desktop to the Quick Launch toolbar. Follow these steps:

1. Open My Computer or Windows Explorer and then open the folder that contains the executable file that starts the program you want to add to the Quick Launch toolbar or that contains a shortcut to this executable file.

2. Drag the program's file icon or shortcut icon to the desired position on the Quick Launch toolbar and then release the mouse button. The mouse pointer indicates where the new button will be inserted with a heavy I-beam cursor at the tip of the pointer.

A button for the program appears at the position of the I-beam in the Quick Launch toolbar.

The following figure shows the Quick Launch toolbar after adding a button for launching Microsoft Word and while still in the process of adding a button for launching Microsoft Excel.

You can delete any of the buttons from the Quick Launch toolbar by right-clicking the button, choosing the <u>D</u>elete command on the shortcut menu, and then choosing the <u>Y</u>es button in the alert box that asks you to confirm the deletion.

Standing up to the Standard Buttons toolbar

The Standard Buttons toolbar (also known simply as the *toolbar*) is the main toolbar that appears in the My Computer, Windows Explorer, and Internet Explorer 4 windows. It is also the most chameleon-like toolbar, because its buttons change to suit the particular type of browsing you are doing. When you browse local files and folders on your computer, the Standard Buttons toolbar contains the following buttons:

✦ **Back:** Returns to the previously browsed folder or Web page.

✦ **Forward:** Returns to the folder or Web page that you browsed right before using the Back button to return to the current page.

✦ **Up:** Moves up one level in the directory structure.

✦ **Cut:** Moves the currently selected files or folders to the Clipboard.

✦ **Copy:** Copies the currently selected files or folders to the Clipboard.

✦ **Paste:** Places files or folders that have been moved or copied into the Clipboard to the current folder (*see* "Copying Files and Folders" in Part III for details).

✦ **Undo:** Eliminates your latest change (blunder?).

✦ **Delete:** Gets rid of the files or folders you've selected (*see* "Deleting Junk" in Part III for details).

✦ **Properties:** Get properties information about the disks, files, or folders you've selected (*see* "Owning up to properties dialog boxes" earlier in this part for details).

✦ **View:** Click repeatedly to rotate through the icon view options or use the attached pull-down menu to select a different icon view for the current window.

When you browse a Web page, whether it's a local HTML document on your hard drive or one located on a Web server somewhere in cyberspace, the Back and Forward buttons that you see when browsing local folders and files are then joined by the following new buttons:

+ **Stop:** Immediately halts the downloading of a Web page that is just taking far too long to come in.

+ **Refresh:** Refreshes the display of the current Web page (which sometimes helps when the contents of the page appear jumbled or incomplete).

+ **Home:** Displays the Web page designated as the start page. This Web page appears each time you launch the Internet Explorer 4 and connect to the Internet.

+ **Search:** Displays the Search Explorer bar for searching the Web (*see* "Searching the Web" in Part III for details).

+ **Favorites:** Displays the Favorites Explorer bar for revisiting favorite Web pages that you've bookmarked (*see* "Adding to Your Favorites" in Part III for details).

+ **History:** Displays the History Explorer bar for revisiting Web pages that you've visited within the last few days or weeks (*see* "Browsing the Web" in Part III for details).

+ **Channels:** Displays the Channels Explorer bar for subscribing to or opening favorite Web channels (*see* "Subscribing to Channels" in Part III for details).

+ **Fullscreen:** Displays the current Web page at full-screen size, retaining just the buttons (with no text) on the Standard Buttons toolbar.

+ **Mail:** Displays a pop-up menu of e-mail options, including Read Mail, New Message, Send a Link, Send Page, and Read News.

+ **Print:** Sends the current Web page to your printer.

+ **Edit:** Opens the current Web page in the Notepad text editor (exposing the *raw* HTML tags).

Customizing the appearance of a toolbar

You can customize the appearance of each toolbar that you display in Windows 98 by changing its position on the desktop (or, in the case of toolbars, its position on the taskbar) or its order at the top of its windows (in the case of the My Computer, Windows Explorer, or Internet Explorer 4 windows). You can also customize a toolbar by modifying its size and the amount of descriptive information that is displayed along with the icons.

When repositioning or resizing a toolbar, keep the following things in mind:

✦ To change the position or length of a toolbar, you drag the toolbar by its sizing handle (the double vertical bar that appears at the very beginning of the toolbar) as soon as the mouse pointer assumes the shape of a double-headed arrow.

✦ When repositioning a toolbar on the Windows taskbar, you can undock the toolbar and locate it somewhere on the Windows desktop. Just drag its sizing handle up and off the taskbar, releasing the mouse button when the pointer reaches the desired position on the desktop, where it then appears in its own toolbar window complete with Close box. You can also dock the toolbar at the top, far left, or far right of the screen by dragging it to the top edge, left edge, or right edge of the screen before you release the mouse button.

✦ After a toolbar is undocked from the Windows taskbar, you can resize the toolbar window, thus rearranging its buttons, by dragging one of its sides or corners. To close the toolbar, click the window's Close box.

✦ To change which row a toolbar occupies at the top of the My Computer, Windows Explorer, or Internet Explorer 4 window, drag the toolbar's sizing handle up or down until the toolbar jumps to its own row or a row occupied by another toolbar.

✦ When more than one toolbar occupies the taskbar or the same row in the My Computer, Windows Explorer, or Internet Explorer 4 window, you can control how many buttons are displayed in each toolbar by changing the toolbar's length. To change the length, drag the appropriate sizing handle(s) to the left or right.

You can identify each of the buttons on the toolbars that appear on the taskbar or at the top of the My Computer, Windows Explorer, or Internet Explorer 4 windows either by displaying the button's ToolTip or by displaying the name of the buttons below or to the immediate right of each button's icon.

To display a button's ToolTip, you simply hover the mouse pointer over the button's icon until the comment box containing the button's text label appears. To display the names of the buttons below or to the right of the icons on the toolbar (or to remove them if they are already displayed), you right-click somewhere on the toolbar (making sure not to click the button itself) and choose the Show Text command on the toolbar's shortcut menu.

In addition to displaying the names of the buttons on a toolbar with the Show Text command, you can display the name of any toolbar on the taskbar. To display the name of the toolbar in front of the first button, right-click somewhere on the toolbar (making sure not to click a button) and then choose the Show Title command on the shortcut menu.

Creating custom toolbars from folders

You can add your own custom toolbars to the Windows taskbar from the folders that you keep on your computer. When you create a custom toolbar from an existing folder, Windows creates buttons for each of the shortcuts and icons that the folder contains.

To create a custom toolbar from a folder, follow these steps:

1. Right-click the taskbar (without clicking any of the buttons or icons it contains) and then choose the Toolbars⇨New Toolbar command on the shortcut menu that appears.

Windows opens the New Toolbar dialog box, where you enter the pathname of the folder to be used in creating the new toolbar.

2. Select the folder whose contents is to be used in creating the new toolbar by opening its folder in the New Toolbar list box, shown in the following figure, or by typing its directory path in the text box at the top.

3. Click the OK button to close the New Toolbar dialog box.

As soon as you close the New Toolbar dialog box, Windows adds the new toolbar, with buttons for each shortcut and icon, to the taskbar. Note that Windows gives the new toolbar the same name as that of the folder you selected, which is automatically displayed along with the names of the buttons.

4. (Optional) To remove the new custom toolbar from the taskbar and place it in its own toolbar window on the desktop or to dock it at the top, left, or right edge of the screen, drag the toolbar's sizing handle to the desired place on the desktop.

5. (Optional) To remove the toolbar's name, right-click somewhere on the toolbar (without clicking one of the buttons) and choose the Sho<u>w</u> Title command on the shortcut menu.

6. (Optional) To remove the name of the buttons from the toolbar, right-click somewhere on the toolbar (without clicking one of the buttons) and choose the Show <u>T</u>ext command on the shortcut menu.

All custom toolbars that you create last only during your current work session. In other words, whenever you close a custom toolbar or restart your computer, the toolbar is automatically erased and you must re-create it by using the steps just outlined if you want access to its buttons.

Windows (The On-Screen Type)

Windows, whether they are Windows system types (such as the My Computer, Windows Explorer, or Control Panel windows) or program windows (such WordPad program window), contain various combinations of controls and features that you use to modify the window and, in the case of program windows, navigate a program.

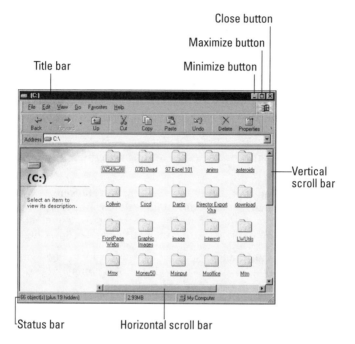

Close button

Maximize button

Title bar   Minimize button

Vertical
scroll bar

Status bar   Horizontal scroll bar

The following list describes the features and controls found on all your typical windows:

✦ **Title bar:** Identifies the program or file in the opened window; also houses the Control menu, which appears when you click the program icon on the left side of the Title bar.

✦ **Menu bar:** Contains the pull-down menus with commands specific to a program (*see* "Messing around with the menu bar" earlier in this part).

✦ **Minimize button:** Shrinks the window down to a button on the taskbar.

✦ **Maximize button:** Zooms the window up to full size; to restore a maximized window to its former size, click the Restore button that replaces the Maximize button.

✦ **Close button:** Closes the window and exits any program running in it.

✦ **Toolbars:** If the window is equipped with other toolbars (like a Standard Buttons bar), these extra toolbars are usually located below the menu bar.

+ **Vertical scroll bar:** Enables you to vertically scroll new parts of the window into view with the up and down arrows or by dragging the scroll button.

+ **Horizontal scroll bar:** Enables you to horizontally scroll new parts of the window into view with the right and left arrows or by dragging the scroll button.

+ **Status bar:** Gives you different sorts of information about the current state of the program.

Here are some basic tips on dealing with the windows you encounter in Windows 98:

+ A window must be active before you can select any of its commands or use any of its features. To activate a window, click anywhere on it. The active window is immediately placed on top of the desktop and its title bar becomes highlighted.

+ You can change the size of a window by dragging its borders with the mouse or by using the Size command (*see* "Moving and Sizing Windows" in Part III).

+ To move a window on the desktop, position the mouse pointer somewhere on the window's title bar and drag the outline to the new location with the mouse.

+ If the window contains a toolbar and you don't have a clue as to what the tool does, point to the tool button, and Windows displays a ToolTip with the tool's name.

See also "Dialog Boxes" earlier in this part for the lowdown on this special type of window.

Windows Desktop

The Windows desktop is the background against which all of the action takes place. Not only does it contain the standard Windows icons (My Computer, Recycle Bin, and the like), the Windows taskbar, and all the shortcuts you've created, but when the View as Web Page option is selected, it also displays all the Active Desktop items to which you've subscribed to (*see* "Active Desktop" earlier in this part and "Adding Active Desktop Items" in Part II for details).

The Desktop shortcut menu, opened by right-clicking any open area of the desktop (above the taskbar), contains the following commands, which enable you to customize the look and feel of the Windows 98 desktop:

✦ **Active Desktop:** Turns the Active Desktop off and on with the View As Web Page command; opens the Display Properties dialog box with the Customize My Desktop command; or updates Active Desktop items with the Update Now command.

✦ **Arrange Icons:** Enables you to arrange the desktop icons by Name, by Type, by Size, or by Date, or you can use Auto Arrange to let Windows 98 decide how to arrange them (*see* "Arranging Icons in a Window" in Part III).

✦ **Line up Icons:** Arranges the icons (by name, in alphabetical order) in neat columns and rows on the desktop.

✦ **Refresh:** Updates icons and Active Desktop items displayed on the desktop.

✦ **Paste:** Creates a shortcut to whatever document you're currently working on and pastes its onto the desktop.

✦ **Paste Shortcut:** Pastes whatever shortcut you've cut or copied to the Clipboard.

✦ **New:** Creates an empty folder, a file of a particular type (such as an Excel file or Word document), a new briefcase (*see* "My Briefcase" earlier in this part), or a new shortcut.

✦ **Properties:** Opens the Display Properties dialog box, where you can change display stuff, like the video settings and windows color combinations (*see* "Display Properties" in Part IV for details).

See "Activating/Deactivating the Active Desktop" in Part II for information on how to switch the Active Desktop on and off and how you can have Windows automatically hide the desktop icons whenever you turn on the Web view.

Windows Explorer

The Windows Explorer enables you to view the contents of any part of your computer system. As with the My Computer and Internet Explorer 4 windows, you can then use the Windows Explorer to open files (and their associated application programs), start programs, or even open Web pages on the Internet or your company's intranet.

The Windows Explorer, however, is most useful when you need to move or copy files to different disks on your computer — or even to networked drives, if you're on a network (*see* "Copying Files and Folders" in Part III for details on how to do this).

To open the Windows Explorer, click the Start button and then choose Programs⇨Windows Explorer. Windows opens an Exploring window (which you see in the following figure) for your disk drive (C:) that is divided into these two panes:

+ The All Folders pane on the left shows an outline view of all the components on your computer system.

+ The Contents area on the right displays the folders and files in whatever component is currently selected in the All Folders pane (also shown on the Address bar at the top of the window).

To select a new part of your system to view in the Contents area pane, simply click the icon for that component in the All Folders pane. An icon in the All Folders pane, with a plus sign connected to it, indicates a sublevel within that icon.

When you click a plus sign, Windows expands the outline, showing all the subfolders within the next level. Note also that when you click the plus sign, it turns to a minus sign, and the next level in the item's hierarchy is displayed. Clicking the minus sign collapses the sublevel to which it is attached, thus condensing the outline.

When the expanded folder/subfolder outline in the All Folders pane (or the icon arrangements in the Contents pane) becomes too large to view in its entirety given the current Explorer window size, vertical and horizontal scroll bars appear as needed, to help you navigate your way through the lists of folders and system components.

If all this hierarchy business is scary — and believe me, many Windows focus groups feel the same way — you can get rid of the All Folders pane by clicking the Close button at the top of the pane. You're then left with just the Contents area pane, which now looks exactly like the My Computer window! The Explorer keeps this appearance until it is closed and reopened, at which time it emerges again (as in the preceding figure) in all its hierarchical glory (*see* "Explorer Bars" earlier in this part for more information).

The Explorer window, like all windows in Windows 98, can be modified in the following ways:

♦ Change the way items are viewed in the Contents area (*see* "Arranging Icons in a Window" in Part III).

♦ Modify the size of the entire Exploring window (*see* "Moving and Resizing Windows" in Part III).

You can resize the panes within the Exploring window. To adjust the size of the All Folders and Contents area panes (relative to each other), position the mouse pointer on the dividing line between the two and then drag right or left when the pointer changes to a double-headed arrow.

Part II

Getting Involved with the Active Desktop

In Windows 98, the Active Desktop represents a first attempt by Microsoft at integrating the local Windows desktop with the World Wide Web on the Internet. As you peruse the entries in this part, you'll soon find out you're definitely NOT dealing with your mother's Windows here!

In this part . . .

- ✔ Turning on and off the Web Page view for the desktop
- ✔ Adding Active Desktop items for your edification and amusement
- ✔ Adding Web pages, folders, and files to your Favorites folder
- ✔ Browsing folders on your local disks, along with Web pages on the Internet
- ✔ Changing the way you select and open objects in Windows in the Folder Options dialog box
- ✔ Conferencing and chatting with NetMeeting and Microsoft Chat
- ✔ Creating a custom Web Page view for a folder on a local disk
- ✔ Searching the Web
- ✔ Sending and receiving e-mail messages with Outlook Express
- ✔ Subscribing to and viewing Active Web channels
- ✔ Viewing TV channels with the TV Viewer
- ✔ Finding out about the Update wizard

Activating/Deactivating the Desktop Web Page View

The Windows 98 desktop consists of three layers, each of which lies on top of the other. On the very top you find the layer with the regular Windows desktop icons (like those for My Computer, Network Neighborhood, and the like). In the middle you find the layer with the Active Desktop items to which you subscribe (which may be just the Internet Explorer Channel bar, if you haven't added any items on your own). On the bottom you find the layer containing whatever image or HTML document, if any, you use as the desktop wallpaper.

You can turn the "active" aspect of the Windows 98 desktop on and off at will by turning on and off the Web Page view. When you turn the Web Page view off, Windows hides the middle layer, which contains all the Active Desktop items (such as the Internet Explorer Channel Bar, as well as any other items to which you subscribe). In addition, if you have made an HTML document into the desktop wallpaper, turning off the Active Desktop also hides the document on the bottom layer. The result is that only the top layer, which has the regular Windows desktop icons, is visible.

The following figure shows the desktop of my computer with the Web Page view turned on. In this figure, you can see the whole shebang: the Windows desktop icons on the left, the Active Desktop items (including the MSNBC weather map, Corbis tripscope, the 3D Java clock, and, of course, the Internet Explorer Channel bar) spreading out from the center toward the right, and, at the top, the Microsoft Windows 98 logo, which is part of the HTML document that is designated as the desktop wallpaper.

Now take a gander at the same desktop after turning off the Web Page view. In the following figure, only the desktop icons (on the top layer) remain the same. Gone are all the Active Desktop icons as well as the HTML document with the Microsoft Windows 98 logo used as wallpaper. In place of the HTML document, you now see a centered JPEG image (of the machine from the movie *Contact*).

Each time you start Windows 98, the Internet Explorer Channel Bar appears on the desktop even when the Web Page view is turned off. Should you then turn on the Web Page view and later turn it off again, however, the Internet Explorer Channel Bar no longer appears on the desktop (as shown in the preceding figure). If you want to remove the Internet Explorer Channel Bar from the desktop when the Web Page view is off without having to switch back and forth, simply position the mouse pointer on the Channel Bar until the title bar appears; then click its Close button.

Turning the desktop Web Page view on and off

As is often the case, Microsoft gives you a couple of ways to turn the desktop Web Page view on and off:

+ Right-click somewhere on the desktop (outside of a desktop icon or Active Desktop item) and choose Active Desktop⇨View as Web Page on the shortcut menu.

+ Click the Start button on the taskbar and then choose Settings⇨Active Desktop⇨View as Web Page on the Start menu.

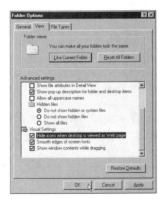 The Windows desktop is not the only Windows element that you can view as a Web page. In fact, any window in Windows 98 (My Computer, Windows Explorer, Control Panel, and so on) can be viewed as a Web page (they didn't call it "Web integration" for nothing). For more on working with Web Page views for folders viewed in the browsing windows, *see* "Browsing folders with Web Page view turned on" later in this part.

Turning the desktop icons off when the Web Page view is on

Depending on how many Active Desktop items you keep on your desktop (*see* "Adding Active Desktop Items" for details), you may want to hide the regular desktop icons anytime you have the desktop Web Page view on. That way, you have much more screen real estate in which to arrange the Active Desktop items without having to worry about any overlapping by the desktop icons on the layer above.

To turn off the display of the desktop icons whenever the desktop Web Page view is turned on, you follow these steps:

1. Open either My Computer or the Windows Explorer.

2. Choose View⇨Folder Options to display the Folder Options dialog box, which you see in the following figure.

3. Click the View tab in the Folder Options dialog box.

4. Scroll down the Advanced Settings list box until you can see the Visual Settings.

5. Click the Hide icons when desktop is viewed as Web page check box to put a check mark in it.

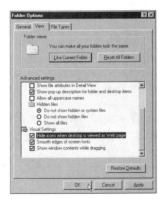

6. Click the OK button to close the Folder Options dialog box and put the new settings into effect.

After you put this new Hide Icons option into effect, all desktop icons automatically disappear each time you turn on the View as Web page setting for the desktop, and they just as automatically reappear whenever you turn this setting off.

But what, you may ask, do I do if I need one of the desktop icons when the Web Page view is on and the icons are not? My suggestion is that you display the desktop toolbar, and maybe even dock it on the left or top of your screen (*see* "Dealing with the desktop toolbar" in Part I for details). That way, you still have plenty of room for your Active Desktop items and easy access to all your desktop icons.

Adding buttons for desktop icons to the Internet Explorer Channel bar

If you don't want to allocate as much desktop space as the desktop toolbar uses, you can access your desktop icons by adding shortcuts to them to the Internet Explorer Channel bar (which is, after all, one of the Active Desktop items that you always see when the Web Page view is on).

To add a shortcut for a particular desktop icon to Internet Explorer Channel bar, drag the icon to the place on the bar where you want its button to appear (indicated by a heavy, black, horizontal I-beam) and release the mouse button (of course, the Hide icons when desktop is viewed as Web page check box must not be selected when you try this technique).

If you drag an icon representing one of the desktop components, such as My Computer or the Recycle Bin, Windows displays an alert box telling you that you cannot move or copy the icon to this location and asking if you want to create a shortcut to it instead. Click the Yes button in this alert box to add a button with a shortcut to this Windows component.

The big drawback to adding desktop icons to the Internet Explorer Channel bar is that you usually can't read the name of the item following the icon on the button (especially if it is a shortcut to the item, in which case the buttons all say Shortcut to, with the rest of the text being cut off).

Moreover, when you open one of the desktop components, such as My Computer or the Recycle Bin, with a button on the Internet Explorer Channel bar, the component opens in the Active Channel viewer (a fancy name for an Internet Explorer 4 window with the full-screen viewing option turned on). The result is that although you have access to the buttons on the Standard Buttons bar (minus their titles), you don't have access to any of the other toolbars, including the menu bar and the sometimes-very-important Address bar. If trying to get your business done in a window that offers you no access to its pull-down menus bothers you at all, you should steer clear of adding buttons for the desktop items to the Internet Explorer Channel bar.

Adding Active Desktop Items

Active Desktop items are smaller, special versions of channel Web pages that reside right on your computer's desktop. Active Desktop items appear whenever the desktop Web Page view is turned on (*see* "Activating/Deactivating the Desktop Web Page View" for details).

Like regular channel pages, Active Desktop items are HTML documents. And, as with channels, when adding Active Desktop items, you must go through a subscription process in which you indicate when and how you want updates made to the contents of the item (*see* "Subscribing to Web Channels" in this part for details).

Unlike regular channel Web pages, whose contents are always viewed in a Web browser (like Internet Explorer 4), the contents of Active Desktop items are displayed on the desktop in their own borderless windows (known as *frames*) without requiring a Web browser (such as Internet Explorer 4) to be running. Not only do Active Desktop items run independently of a Web browser, but you also can move and resize their windows around the Windows desktop as your needs and design sense dictate.

Subscribing to an Active Desktop item

When you first start using Windows 98, only a single Active Desktop item — the Internet Explorer Channel bar — appears on your Active Desktop. After that, it's up to you to go out and subscribe to any additional Active Desktop goodies that you want adorning your desktop.

One method for adding an Active Desktop item is by subscribing to a new Active Web Channel. Many times, as part of the subscription process, the channel's subscription page gives you the option (usually in the form of an Add to Active Desktop button) of adding an Active Desktop item directly to your desktop.

Another, more surefire, method for adding an Active Desktop item is by installing it from the Microsoft Active Desktop gallery. To connect to this gallery and install a new Active Desktop item, you follow these steps:

1. Right-click the desktop to display its shortcut menu.

2. Choose Active Desktop⇨Customize my Desktop to open the Display Properties dialog box, shown in the following figure, and then click the Web tab.

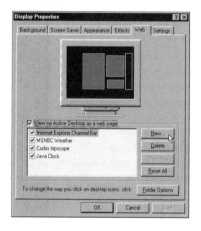

3. Click the New button in the Display Properties dialog box to open the New Active Desktop Item dialog box, shown in the following figure.

4. Click the Yes button in the New Active Desktop Item dialog box to close the New Active Desktop Item and Display Properties dialog boxes and have Internet Explorer open the Desktop Gallery Web page on the Microsoft Web site, as shown in the following figure.

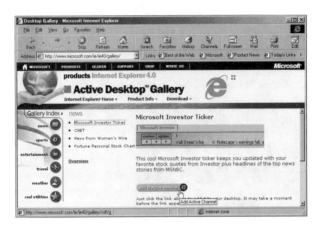

This Web page contains links for downloading all sorts of nifty Active Desktop items, from the MSNBC Investor ticker to a 3D Java clock. Because new Active Desktop items are added to this gallery all the time, you may want to subscribe to this page (*see* "Subscribing to favorite Web pages" later in this part) so that you are automatically notified when new items are added. Or, at the very least, you may want to add the page to your favorites (which you can do in a snap, by dragging the icon for this Web page from the Address bar to the Favorites button on the Standard Buttons bar).

5. To open a new Web page containing the desktop item, click the hyperlink for the Active Desktop item that you want to add. Then, after reading over the details on the item, click the Add to Active Desktop button to open the Add item to Active Desktop(TM) dialog box, which you see in the following figure.

6. Click the OK button in the Add Item to Active Desktop(TM) dialog box to accept the default subscription options, or click the Customize button and modify the settings as required (*see* "Subscribing to Web Channels" later in this part for help with the custom settings).

After you close the Add to Active Desktop(TM) dialog box, a Download Progress dialog box appears, keeping you informed of the download progress of the Active Desktop item you selected. When the Download Progress dialog box disappears, you can return to the desktop to check out your new toy.

7. Click the Close box in the Internet Explorer 4 window to return to the desktop.

8. If you don't see your new Active Desktop item right away, right-click on an unoccupied part of the desktop to display the shortcut menu and then choose the Refresh command.

Moving and resizing items on the desktop

After you install a new Active Desktop item, you can move and resize it much as you do any other less-than-full-size window on the desktop. To move an Active Desktop item, position the mouse pointer somewhere over the item until a gray title bar, blank except for a pop-up button in the upper-left corner and a Close box in the upper-right corner, appears on the top of the item. Then drag the Active Desktop item by this title bar to its new position on the desktop and move the mouse pointer off of the Active Desktop item.

To resize an Active Desktop item, position the mouse pointer on one of its borders until one of the resizing pointers (either a horizontal, vertical, or diagonal double-headed arrow) appears. Then drag the border or borders of the desktop item until the item is the size you want.

Modifying the subscription settings or removing an item from the desktop

To change the settings or to unsubscribe from an Active Desktop item, you need to open its Properties dialog box. To open this dialog box, position the mouse pointer somewhere over the item until its title bar appears and then click the pop-up button (the one with the downward-pointing arrow) and select the Properties command to open the Properties dialog box for that desktop item.

To unsubscribe from the Active Desktop item, click the Unsubscribe button on the Subscription tab. To change when and how the item's content is updated, click the Receiving and/or Schedule tab and change the settings accordingly. Note that when you unsubscribe from an Active Desktop item, you delete the item entirely from your computer's desktop, and the only way to bring it back is by going through the subscription process all over again.

To temporarily remove an Active Desktop item from the desktop without deleting it (that is, without unsubscribing from it), display the title bar for the Active Desktop item and then click its Close box in the upper-right corner.

You can also unsubscribe from an Active Desktop item, or just temporarily close the item, from the Display Properties dialog box (which you open by right-clicking the desktop and choosing Properties from the shortcut menu). To close the desktop item, choose the Web tab and then remove the check mark from the item's check box in the Items on the Active Desktop list box. To unsubscribe from the item, select the item in this list box and then click the Delete button.

Adding to Your Favorites

You keep bookmarks for all of your often-used Folders and files, as well as for often-revisited Web pages, in the Favorites folder. Bookmarks for folders, files, and pages that you store in this folder are available from any of three browsing windows: My Computer, Windows Explorer, and Internet Explorer 4.

To access and open an item whose bookmark is stored in the Favorites folder, you have a choice between choosing the bookmark from the Favorites pull-down menu or from the Favorites Explorer bar (*see* "Explorer Bars" in Part I for details).

When you first start adding to the Favorites folder, you will find that it already contains certain subfolders. The Favorites folder contains a subfolder for the Channels, Links, My Documents, and the Personal folders on your hard drive. In addition, the Favorites folder may contain a subfolder with your computer manufacturer's favorite Web sites (called something like "XYZ" Corporation Recommended Sites) and, if you imported bookmarks from the address book created with another Web browser's e-mail program into Outlook Express, a subfolder called Imported Bookmarks.

Follow these steps to add a bookmark to a folder, file, or Web page to your Favorites folder:

1. Open one of the browsing windows (My Computer, Windows Explorer, or Internet Explorer 4) and then select the folder, file, or Web page for which you want to add a bookmark in your Favorites folder.

When adding bookmarks for local folders, be sure to open the folder and verify that the folder name appears at the end of the path name on the Address bar. When adding bookmarks for local files (including local HTML documents), just select the file without opening it and make sure that the filename appears at the end of the path name on the Address bar. When adding bookmarks for Web pages on the Internet, open the Web page (the URL of the page appears on the Address bar).

2. Choose Favorites⇨Add to Favorites to open the Add Favorite dialog box.

The Add Favorite dialog box contains a Name text box with the name of the folder or file, or the title of the Web page that you are adding to the Favorites folder.

3. (Optional) If you want a different bookmark description to appear on the Favorites menu, edit the name that currently appears in the Name text box.

4. (Optional) To add the bookmark in a subfolder of the Favorites folder, click the Create In button to expand the Add to Favorites dialog box and then click the subfolder's icon. To add the bookmark to a new folder, select the icon of the folder in which the new folder is to be inserted and then click the New Folder button in the expanded Add Favorite dialog box, which you see in the following figure. Then enter the folder name in the Create New Folder dialog box and click OK.

5. Click OK to close the Add Favorite dialog box and to add the bookmark to the folder, file, or Web page to the Favorites menu of the three browsing windows (My Computer, Windows Explorer, and Internet Explorer 4).

If you want to add a bookmark to the current Web page to your Favorites folder, you can do so simply by dragging the Web page icon (that appears before the page's URL in the Address bar) to the Favorites button on the Standard Buttons toolbar. If you later decide that you want the bookmark to appear in a subfolder of the Favorites folder, you can then move it to the desired subfolder (*see* "Organizing your favorites" for details).

Opening an item in your Favorites

After you add a folder, file, or Web page to your Favorites folder (or one of its subfolders), you can open the item simply by selecting its bookmark, either from the Favorites pull-down menu or from the Favorites Explorer bar.

To select a bookmark from the Favorites pull-down menu in the My Computer, Windows Explorer, or Internet Explorer 4 window, you click Favorites on the menu bar and then click the name of the bookmark on the Favorites menu. If the bookmark is located in a subfolder of the Favorites, you need to drag down to the subfolder's icon to open its submenu, where you can click the desired bookmark.

To select a bookmark from the Favorites Explorer bar, open the Explorer bar by choosing View⇨Explorer Bar⇨Favorites on the window's pull-down menus (in Internet Explorer 4, just click the Favorites button on the Standard Buttons toolbar), and then click the bookmark's hyperlink. If the bookmark is located in a subfolder of Favorites, click the subfolder to expand the list and display its bookmarks and then click the hyperlink for the book-mark to the folder, file, or Web page you want to open.

Subscribing to favorite Web pages

When you add a bookmark to a Web page, you can also subscribe to the page so that you are notified that the contents of the page have been updated or so that the updated page is automatically downloaded for offline viewing. If the contents of the page have been updated, a small, red starburst — which Microsoft refers to as a *gleam* — appears in the upper-left corner of the Web file's icon.

This kind of Web page subscription is useful when you're marking a Web page whose contents change frequently (like a page of an online catalog where the merchandise and prices are in constant flux) and you don't want to have to keep revisiting the page just to see if anything new has been added.

To subscribe to a Web page, follow these steps:

1. Open the Web page you want to bookmark and concurrently subscribe to in My Computer, Windows Explorer, or Internet Explorer 4.

2. Choose Favorites⇨Add to Favorites on the pull-down menus to open the Add Favorite dialog box.

3. Beneath the question Would you also like to sub-scribe to this page? click the Yes, but tell me only when this page is updated radio button if you want to be notified only when the contents of the page change. Click the Yes, notify me of updates and download the page for offline viewing radio button to have the new contents automatically downloaded as well.

4. (Optional) To customize the subscription settings for the Web page so that you receive an e-mail message whenever the page changes (in addition to having the page's icon take on the gleam), click the Customize button and then click the Yes, send an e-mail message to the following address radio button. Finally, click the Next button in the first dialog box in the Subscription wizard and then the Finish button in the second dialog box.

5. (Optional) To add the bookmark to the Web page in a subfolder of the Favorites folder, click the Create In button to expand the Add to Favorites dialog box. Then click the subfolder's icon. To add the bookmark to a new folder, select the icon of the folder in which the new folder is to be inserted and then click the New Folder button in the expanded Add Favorite dialog box. Next, enter the folder name in the Create New Folder dialog box and click OK.

6. Click OK to close the Add Favorite dialog box and add the bookmark to the Web page to the Favorites menu of the three browsing windows (My Computer, Windows Explorer, and Internet Explorer 4) and complete the subscription to the Web page.

A few Web pages purposely block you from subscribing to them (wonder what they've got to hide?). When this is the case, both the Yes, but tell me only when this page is updated and the Yes, notify me of updates and download the page for offline viewing radio buttons are dimmed.

If, after adding just a plain old bookmark to a Web page, you decide that you want to subscribe to it, you can still do so. Just right-click the bookmark on the Favorites pull-down menu or Explorer bar and choose the Properties command on the shortcut menu. This action opens the Properties dialog box for the book-mark. Then click the Subscription tab in the Properties dialog box, followed by clicking the Subscribe button and selecting the desired subscription options (as discussed in the preceding steps) in the Subscribe Favorite dialog box.

For more on subscriptions, *see* "Subscribing to Channels" later in this part.

Organizing your Favorites

Many times, you will find yourself going along, adding bunches of bookmarks to your pet folders, files, and Web pages without ever bothering to create them in particular subfolders. Then, to your dismay, you find yourself confronted with a seemingly endless list of unrelated bookmarks every time you open the Favorites submenu or Explorer bar.

Fortunately, Windows makes it easy to reorganize even the most chaotic of bookmark lists in just a few, easy steps:

1. Open up one of the three browsing windows (My Computer, Windows Explorer, or Internet Explorer 4) and then choose Favorites⇨Organize Favorites to open the Organize Favorites dialog box.

The list box of the Organize Favorites dialog box shows all the subfolders, followed by all the bookmarks in the Favorites folder.

2. To move bookmarks into one of the subfolders of Favorites, select their icons and then click the Move button to open the Browse for Folder dialog box. Click the destination folder in the Browse for Folder dialog box and then click the OK button.

Use the following options in the Organize Favorites dialog box to create new folders to hold your bookmarks, to rename bookmarks, or even to get rid of unwanted bookmarks:

✦ To create a new folder, click the Create New Folder icon and type a new name for the folder icon; then press Enter.

✦ To rename a link to a favorite page, channel, or Web subscription, click its icon to select it, click the Rename button, edit the description, and then press Enter.

✦ To delete a link to a favorite page, or to unsubscribe from a channel or Web subscription, click its icon and then click the Delete button. Choose Yes in the Confirm File Delete dialog box when it asks whether you're sure that you want to send the particular favorite page, channel, or Web subscription to the Recycle Bin.

Don't delete or rename the Links folder in the Organize Favorites dialog box. Internet Explorer 4 needs the Links folder so that it knows what buttons to display on the Links bar.

You can also use the drag-and-drop method to do some quick reordering of the bookmarks in the Organize Favorites dialog box. Just drag the bookmark to the desired subfolder in the list box and release the mouse button.

Note that you can also use drag-and-drop in the Favorites Explorer bar to change the order of the bookmarks within a particular folder or to move bookmarks to new folders. Just open the Favorites Explorer bar in one of the three browsing windows (choose View⇨Explorer Bar⇨Favorites) and then use one of these techniques:

✦ To open one of the folders on the Explorer bar to display the folder's contents, click its folder icon. Internet Explorer then displays a series of icons for each of the subfolders and bookmarks it contains. To close a folder to hide its contents, click the folder icon again.

✦ To move a bookmark to a new position in its folder, drag its icon up or down until you reach the desired position. As you drag, you see where the item will be inserted by the display of a heavy, horizontal I-beam between the bookmarks. You also see where you *cannot* move the icon because of the display of the international No-No symbol.

✦ To move a bookmark's icon to a different (existing) folder, drag the bookmark icon to the folder icon. When a plus sign (+) appears at the mouse pointer, you can drop the icon into the highlighted folder.

Browsing Folders on a Local Disk

You can use any of the three Windows 98 browsing windows (My Computer, Windows Explorer, or Internet Explorer 4) to browse the contents of the drives attached to your computer. These disks can be in local drives, such as your floppy drive (A:), hard drive (C:), or CD-ROM drive (D:). If your computer is on a Local Area Network (LAN), these disks can be disks on remote drives to which you have access, such as a network E:, F:, or G: drive.

When you browse folders and files on a local drive (as opposed to browsing Web pages on the Internet), the Windows icon (you know the disintegrating four-pane window with the clouds behind it thing) appears in the button on the far right of the menu bar. When you browse Web pages, the icon for this button automatically changes to the E icon used by the Internet Explorer. Note, however, that clicking this button in a browsing window connects you to the Microsoft Internet Start page on the Internet, regardless of which icon currently appears.

Browsing folders with Internet Explorer 4

Although browsing folders with My Computer and Windows Explorer is more direct (because these windows both sport icons for the drives attached to your computer — *see* "My Computer" and "Windows Explorer" in Part I), you can just as well as browse folders and open files in Internet Explorer 4. To do this kind of local browsing with Internet Explorer, follow these simple steps:

1. Click the cursor in the Address bar to select the current URL or file path and then type the letter of the disk drive whose folders you want to see. If the AutoComplete feature correctly completes the drive specification by adding the obligatory colon and backslash (as in D:\), press Enter. If AutoComplete does not correctly complete the drive specification, type a colon (:) and, if necessary, a backslash before you press Enter. If you know the path of the particular folder whose files and subfolders you want to display, don't stop with entering the drive letter; go ahead and type the entire file path (in most cases, AutoComplete enters the complete name of the folder as soon as you type enough characters to trigger recognition of the folder name).

Note that as soon as you enter a drive letter or directory path in the Address bar, the buttons on the Standard Buttons bar change to those buttons that you need for local (as opposed to Web) browsing (*see* "Standing up to the Standard Buttons toolbar" in Part I).

2. (Optional) To change the view of the folders and files in the browser window, choose the desired view option (Large Icons, Small Icons, List, or Details) from the View pull-down menu or from the pop-up menu attached to the View button (located at the end of the Standard Buttons bar).

3. To open a folder displayed in the browser window to see its subfolders and files, click the folder's hyperlink (use Web-style folder selection) or double-click the folder's icon.

4. To return to browsing Web pages on the Internet after you finish browsing folders on a disk, click the drop-down button attached to the Address bar and then click the Internet icon on the pop-up menu. Otherwise, click the Home button or select a Web page on the Favorites pull-down menu.

When browsing folders with Internet Explorer 4, remember that you can use the Back and Forward buttons to retrace your path through various levels of folders, and you can click the Up button to display the folders and files in the next level up in the file path hierarchy.

Browsing folders with Web Page view turned on

Windows 98 supports a new folder view called Web Page view. When you turn this view on (by choosing View⇨as Web Page) in one of the browsing windows, vital statistics appear in an info panel on the left side of the window each time you select a particular file or folder icon. These statistics include the folder or file name, the last date modified, and, in the case of files, the file type and size in kilobytes. Moreover, when you select an application file, like a Microsoft Word or Excel document, the name of the person who authored the document also appears in the info panel, and when you select a graphics file whose format Windows 98 can decipher or an HTML document, a thumbnail of the image or page appears as well.

The following figure shows the Windows 98 Explorer after selecting the Graphic Images folder in the All Folders pane, turning on Web Page view, and selecting a file containing a GIF graphic image in the contents pane. Note that in addition to vital statistics (filename, type, last date modified, and size), a thumbnail preview of the graphic appears in the info panel in the contents pane.

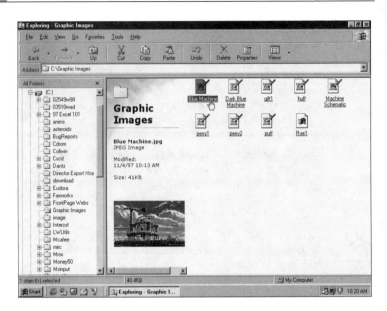

Browsing folders with thumbnail view turned on

When browsing folders that contain numerous graphics or Web pages (for example, the pages that you are developing for your own Web site on the Internet), you can add a thumbnail view to the folder's properties and then use this thumbnail view to display the contents of graphic files and Web pages as thumbnail images.

Before you can use the thumbnail view when browsing the contents of a folder, you must add the thumbnail view to the folder's properties, as follows:

1. Open one of the three browsing windows (My Computer, Windows Explorer, or Internet Explorer 4) and then open the drive and folder that contains the folder to which you want to add the thumbnail view.

2. Right-click the folder's icon and choose Properties from the shortcut menu to open the Properties dialog box for that folder.

3. Click the Enable thumbnail view check box on the General tab of the folder's Properties dialog box and then click OK.

After you enable the thumbnail view for the folder, you can turn it on by taking these steps:

1. Open the folder for which you enabled the thumbnail view in the My Computer, Windows Explorer, or Internet Explorer 4 window.

2. Choose View➪Thumbnails or click the drop-down button attached to the Views button on the Standard Buttons bar and then choose Thumbnails from its pop-up menu.

To turn off the thumbnail view for a folder, just select another view (such as Large Icons or List) on the View pull-down menu or the Views button pop-up menu. (You don't have to go to the trouble of disabling the thumbnail view in the folder's Properties dialog box.)

The Web Page view and thumbnail view are mutually exclusive. When the Web Page view is on and you choose Thumbnails from the View pull-down menu or the Views button pop-up menu, Windows automatically turns off the as Web Page setting. Likewise, if you are using thumbnail view and then choose as Web Page from the View pull-down menu or the Views button pop-up menu, Windows turns off the Thumbnails setting.

Browsing Web Pages

Windows 98 lets you browse Web pages not only with Internet Explorer 4 but with My Computer and Windows Explorer as well. (You may want to get rid of the All Folders pane, however, when browsing Web pages in the Windows Explorer by clicking the Fullscreen button or by choosing View➪Explorer Bar➪None.)

There are two basic steps involved with browsing a Web page in the three Windows 98 browsing windows:

✦ Connecting to the Internet

✦ Going to the Web page

Connecting to the Internet

You connect to the Internet either with a dial-up connection using a modem directly connected to your computer or with a connection to a LAN that is itself connected to the Internet through some sort of high-speed telephone line, like a T1 or T3.

When you connect to the Internet via a dial-up connection (as you normally do at home), your modem must call up an Internet service provider (ISP), such as AT&T WorldNet, or a bulletin board service such as America Online (AOL), whose high-speed telephone lines and fancy switching equipment provide you (for a fee) with access to the Internet and all its online services.

When you connect to the Internet via a LAN (as you normally would in a large corporation or at a university), you don't have to do anything special to get connected to the Internet: You have

Internet access any time you turn on your computer and launch the Internet Explorer.

For more information on how to get connected to the Internet, *see* "Online Services" in Part I and "Connecting to the Internet" in Part II of my *Internet Explorer 4 For Windows For Dummies Quick Reference,* published by IDG Books Worldwide, Inc.

Visiting Web pages

Whenever you launch Internet Explorer 4, it automatically attempts to go to the Web page whose address is listed as the home page on the General tab of its Internet Options dialog box (which you open by choosing View➪Internet Options). The same is true if you click the Internet Explorer icon in My Computer (available on the Address bar's drop-down menu) or the All Folders pane of Windows Explorer.

If your computer is configured to use a dial-up connection, Windows automatically begins the process of connecting to your ISP, based on your current dial-up settings. If Windows can't connect to the home page (either because of heavy traffic on the Web site or technical difficulties with site's ISP or your ISP — so much can go wrong!), it displays an alert box with an obscure error message, whereupon Internet Explorer 4 displays a Web page called about:NavigationCanceled in the Address bar (*see* "Launching Internet Explorer 4" in Part I for more on this).

After the connection is made and the home page is displayed in the browsing window, you are free to begin browsing other pages on the World Wide Web by doing any of the following:

✦ Entering the Uniform Resource Locator (URL) of the Web page in the Address bar and pressing Enter

✦ Clicking hyperlinks on the currently displayed Web page that take you to other Web pages, either on the same Web site or on another Web site

✦ Selecting a bookmarked Web page that appears on the Favorites menu or Explorer bar, or one that you've recently visited on the History Explorer bar (*see* "Adding to Your Favorites" earlier in this part for details on how to add Web pages to the Favorites menu)

✦ Using one of the many Web search engines to display hyperlinks for the home pages of Web sites that might possibly fit some search criteria, such as "IRA investments" or, better yet, "Hawaiian vacations" (*see* "Searching the Web" later in this part for details on searching)

Using AutoComplete to fill in a Web site's URL in the Address bar

Of all the methods for browsing pages on the Web just mentioned, none are quite as bad as having to type in the URL addresses with their **http://** and their **www** something or other **.com**'s in the Address bar. To help eliminate errors in typing and speed up this tedious typing process, Windows employs a feature called AutoComplete. This nifty feature looks at whatever few characters of the URL address you type in the Address bar and, based on them, attempts to fill out the missing characters that it thinks you are about to enter.

For example, if you click the cursor in the Address bar and then replace the current address with the letter **h**, AutoComplete enters

```
ttp://
```

so that the Address bar contains `http://` (the beginning of all URLs on the World Wide Web). Note that all characters added by AutoComplete are automatically highlighted.

To accept the characters entered by AutoComplete, you press the → key to move the cursor beyond them, thus deselecting them. If you don't want to accept the characters added by AutoComplete, you just keep on typing as though nothing had been added to the Address bar.

As you continue to type, AutoComplete suggests possible matches to the URL you are entering. When AutoComplete guesses correctly and successfully completes the address of the Web page you want to visit, press Enter to have Internet Explorer 4 take you there.

The AutoComplete feature also helps when you browse folders on a disk.

Browsing Web pages offline

With the advent of channels and Web page subscriptions comes the appearance of so-called *offline* browsing (as opposed to *online* browsing, which indicates being connecting to the Internet). Because you can set up channels and Web site subscriptions so that updated Web pages are automatically downloaded to your hard drive (normally, during the wee hours when you're safely tucked in your beddy-bye and only wild-eyed nerds are surfing the Net), you can use offline browsing to view the updated Web contents with Internet Explorer 4 at your leisure.

This kind of offline browsing is especially beneficial when you're using a laptop computer and can't get connected to the Internet (as when you're in transit on a bus, train, or plane). It can also come in handy when you rely on a relatively slow dial-up connection (as with 28.8 or 33.3 Kbps modems) to the Internet, enabling you to download Web content during nonpeak hours and browse it with maximum efficiency during the peak surfing hours (thereby totally avoiding the "World Wide Wait").

To turn offline browsing on and off, you choose File⇨Work Offline from the browsing window's pull-down menus. Note that after you put the browsing window in offline mode, it remains in this work mode until you restart your computer. In other words, if you shut down the browsing window and then launch it again during the same work session, it will open up in offline mode. If you decide that you want to do some serious online surfing, you need to start by choosing the File⇨Work Offline command to turn off the offline mode.

When offline mode is on (indicated by a check mark in front of the Work Offline command on the File menu), Windows will not attempt to connect to the Internet, and you can only browse pages stored locally on your computer, such as those that have been downloaded into the *cache* on your computer's hard drive. Also known as the Temporary Internet Files, the cache contains all Web pages and their components that are downloaded when you subscribe to Web sites or channels.

 When you browse a Web site offline from a local disk, you have none of the wait often associated with browsing online when connected to the Internet. You may also find, however, that some of the links, especially those to pages on another Web site that you haven't subscribed to, are not available for viewing. The browsing window lets you know when a link is not available by adding the international No or "Don't" symbol (you know, the circle with a backslash in it) to the hand cursor.

If you persist and click a hyperlink to a page that has not been downloaded with the hand-plus-Don't-symbol cursor, the browsing window displays a URL Not Found in Offline Mode dialog box.

This dialog box informs you that the address of the page (URL) is not available offline and gives you a choice between staying offline or connecting to the Internet and downloading the most up-to-date version of the Web page. Click the Connect button in the URL Not Found in Offline Mode dialog box to get on the Internet and download the page (whereupon, you must then choose File⇨Work Offline again to get back to surfing in Offline mode). Click the Stay Offline button to close the alert box and continue browsing in Offline mode.

Most of the time when browsing offline, you do your local Web surfing in one of two ways:

✦ Visit updated Web pages stored in the cache as channels to which you subscribe. You open these pages by selecting them from the Channel Explorer bar opened by clicking the Channels button or by choosing F̲avorites⇨Channels (*see* "Viewing Active Channels" in this part for details).

✦ Revisit Web pages stored in the cache as part of the History. You open these pages by selecting them from the History Explorer bar, which you open by clicking the History button.

In addition to using these two browsing methods, you can open Web pages that are stored in folders on local disks, such as the hard drive or a CD-ROM in your CD-ROM drive. The easiest way to open these pages is by selecting the drive letter in the Address bar (*see* "Browsing Folders on a Local Disk" in this part for details). You can also open a local Web page with the Open dialog box (choose F̲ile⇨O̲pen or press Ctrl+O).

Changing the Folder Options for Windows 98

You can use the Folder Options dialog box to modify the default Active Desktop and Web Page view setting, Folder Options also lets you change how you select and open folder and file icons, what file information appears in the browsing windows, and which programs are associated with what file types.

You can open the Folder Options dialog box in one of two ways:

✦ Choose V̲iew⇨Folder O̲ptions from the pull-down menus in any of the three browsing windows (My Computer, Windows Explorer, or Internet Explorer 4).

✦ Click the Start button on the Windows taskbar and then choose S̲ettings⇨F̲olders & Icons from the Start menu.

Changing the way you select and open icons

The General tab of the Folder Options dialog box, shown in the following figure, is where you change the Active Desktop and Web Page view default settings, and also where you change the way you select and open desktop and windows icons with the mouse. The General tab contains the following three style options:

✦ **Web style:** Enables all Web-related content on the Active Desktop, enables the Web Page view for all folders with HTML content, and makes all your folders and icons look and act like hyperlinks on a Web page, so that you only have to point to them to select them and then single-click to open them.

✦ **Classic style:** Disables all Web-related content on the Active Desktop, disables the Web Page view for all folders with HTML content, and makes all your folders and icons look and act like they did on the "classic" Windows 95 desktop, so that you need to click to select them and double-click to open them.

✦ **Custom, based on settings you choose:** Enables you to select a blend of the classic and Web style features for a truly personalized setup. Click the Settings button to the immediate right of this radio button to open the Custom Settings dialog box and then choose the settings to customize, as described in the following paragraphs.

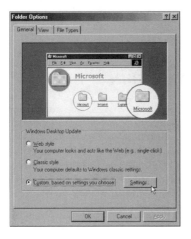

When you open the Custom Settings dialog box (which you see in the following figure) by choosing the Custom, based on settings you choose radio button and then clicking the Settings button, you can customize Folder Option settings in the following four areas:

✦ **Active Desktop:** Choose the Enable all web-related content on my desktop radio button to activate the Active Desktop so that all Active Desktop items and any HTML document used as wallpaper appear on the Windows desktop (*see* "Active Desktop" in Part I for details). Choose the Use Windows classic desktop radio button to turn off the Active Desktop so that all desktop items and any HTML wallpaper disappear.

✦ **Browse folder as follows:** Choose the Open each folder in the same window radio button to have the contents of each subfolder you open in My Computer replace the contents of the folder in which it resides. Choose the Open each folder in its own window radio button to have the contents displayed in a separate, new My Computer window.

✦ **View Web Content in Folders:** Choose the For all folders with HTML content radio button to have Web Page views turned on for all folders that have them (*see* "Creating a Custom Web Page View for a Folder" later in this part for details). Choose the Only for folders where I select "as Web Page" (View Menu) radio button to have Web Page views for folders appear only when you choose View⇨as Web Page.

✦ **Click Items As Follows:** Choose the Single-click to open item (point to select) radio button to select and open folder and file icons as though they were hyperlinks. Choose Double-click to open an item (single-click to select) to select and open them in the classic single- and double-click manner. When you select the Single-click to open item (point to select) radio button, you have a choice between the Underline icon titles consistent with my browser settings radio button and the Underline icon titles only when I point at them radio button. Choose the former radio button when you want the titles normally to appear underlined (making them appear like hyperlinks on a Web page). Choose the latter radio button when you want this hyperlink effect to appear when you position the mouse pointer somewhere on the associated icon.

Changing the View options

The View tab of the Folder Options dialog box (which you see in the following figure) enables you to change a wide variety of settings that affect where and how folders and files appear in the three browsing windows (My Computer, Windows Explorer, and Internet Explorer 4), as well as a few visual settings that affect the look of the entire Windows desktop.

Check out the following list for a quick rundown on changing these settings:

✦ **Remember each folder's view settings:** Remove the check mark from this item if you don't want Windows to use the individual view settings (such as what size icon to use or whether or not to turn on the Web Page view) that you assign to a folder when displaying its contents in one of the three browsing windows.

✦ **Display the full path in title bar:** Add a check mark to this item if you want the full directory path displayed in the Address bar for the folder you have open in one of the three browsing windows.

✦ **Hide file extensions for known file types:** Remove the check mark from this item to display the file extension as part of the file name in the Address bar of the three browsing windows for all recognized file types (*see* "Changing the File Type Options" in this part for details).

✦ **Show Map Network Drive button in toolbar:** Add a check mark to this item if you want a Map Network Drive button to be added to the Standard Buttons bar of the three browsing windows, which you then can use to mount one of the networked drives to which you have access onto your computer system.

✦ **Show file attributes in detail view:** Add a check mark to this item if you want a list of each file's attributes added to the other stats that you see when you choose Details on the View menu or the Views button pop-up menu.

✦ **Show pop-up description for folder and desktop items:** Remove the check mark from this item if you no longer want to be bothered by ToolTips appearing in comment boxes when you select folder, file, and desktop icons.

✦ **Allow all uppercase names:** Add a check mark to this item if you want filenames that were entered in uppercase letters to appear that way in the three browsing windows. When this check box isn't selected (which is the default setting), all filenames appear in lowercase with an initial cap regardless of how you entered the filename.

✦ **Hidden files:** By default, Windows selects the Do not show hidden or system files radio button as the Hidden files setting. To display system files in the three browsing windows without including files that use the Hidden attribute, choose the Do not show hidden files radio button. To display all files, even those with the Hidden attribute, choose the Show all files radio button.

✦ **Hide icons when desktop is viewed as Web page:** Add a check mark to this item if you want the desktop icons to disappear magically when you turn on the Web Page view for the desktop, only to reappear when you turn off the Web Page view (*see* "Activating/Deactivating the Active Desktop" in this part for details).

✦ **Smooth edges of screen fonts:** Add a check mark to this item if you want the characters in windows to not look so jagged. Note that although turning on this setting makes your screen a might prettier, it also requires more system resources, which may result in (oh no!) slower response times and longer waits when refreshing a screen.

✦ **Show window contents while dragging:** Remove the check mark from this item if you don't care to see the entire contents of each window as you drag it to a new position on the screen. Deselecting this setting can speed up this type of operation on slower computers.

Changing the File Type options

The File Types tab of the Folder Options dialog box enables you to specify or modify the associations between specific types of files and which programs open them. And for you really savvy Windows people, this tab enables you to edit the actions that Windows undertakes when you open the icon for a particular file.

When you select the File Types tab in the Folder Options dialog box, you see a list box showing all the registered file types on your computer system. To see what filename extension, MIME type (Multipurpose Internet mail extension used to identify any file type other than text), and program (for automatic launching when you open the file) is associated with a particular file type, click the file type in the Registered file types list box.

If you are sufficiently technically inclined, you can even add a new file type with the New Type button or edit an existing type by selecting it in the Registered file types list box and then clicking the Edit button.

Communicating with NetMeeting

Microsoft NetMeeting is a premier online conferencing tool that incorporates Internet "telephone" calls, online chat sessions, whiteboard sessions (where you get to draw with others on a shared whiteboard), and collaborative document editing, as well as video conferencing. Of course, you need the necessary hardware (microphone, external speakers, and video camera, to name a few), and you must have a mighty fast Internet connection to make much good use of the tools.

You can start NetMeeting in one of two ways:

✦ From within any of the three browsing windows (My Computer, Windows Explorer, or Internet Explorer 4), choose Go⇨Internet Call.

✦ From anywhere in Windows, click the Start button on the taskbar and then choose Programs⇨Microsoft NetMeeting from the Start menu.

The first time you open NetMeeting, a wizard appears and takes you through a registration and microphone test in which you enter your name, e-mail address, city, and state, and tune your audio settings by speaking a few sentences into the microphone attached to your computer.

After that initial encounter with the wizard, when you start NetMeeting, the program opens the NetMeeting window, which is your master control station for all Internet calls and conferencing activities.

Placing a conference call

In order to facilitate NetMeeting conferences, Microsoft maintains directory servers that list users who have logged on to the server and are available for conference calls. By default, NetMeeting is set up to check in with the Microsoft directory service when you start the program. However, you can select a different directory service (by using the Directory Server name setting on the Calling tab of the Options dialog box); in fact, your network administrator may have set up a directory service for your local network.

After NetMeeting makes contact with a directory, you can place a call to someone listed on that directory simply by double-clicking a name in the directory list. NetMeeting places a call to that person, using the default settings. If you want to specify call settings, you can click the Call button on the toolbar or choose Call⇨New Call (or press Ctrl+N). This action opens the New Call dialog box, where you can specify (in the Address drop-down list box) the e-mail address, computer name, network address, or the telephone number of the modem to which you want to connect.

After you make a call and the other conference participant accepts the connection, you can talk with each other as you would when conducting a telephone call. The sound quality isn't as good as a telephone connection, and you may need to take turns talking because some sound cards don't allow both the microphone and speakers to work at the same time. Still, the system works pretty well. (If you and the other conference participants have those nifty little video cameras attached to your computers, you can even see whom you're talking to.)

Chatting with the keyboard

The Chat window enables you to type a message and have it appear simultaneously on the screens of the other participants. To use NetMeeting's Chat feature, follow these steps:

1. Choose Tools⇨Chat on the NetMeeting Menu bar (or press Ctrl+T) to open the Chat window on your desktop. That action also opens a Chat window on each of the other conference participants' screens.

2. Type a message into the Message text box at the bottom of the Chat window.

3. To send your message to all the other conference participants, press Enter or click the large Send button in the lower-right corner of the Chat window.

Your message appears in the upper panel of the Chat window of all conference participants. Other participants can send messages in the same way. Each message in the Chat window is preceded by the name of the participant who sent the message.

Using the Whiteboard

The Whiteboard window is another NetMeeting resource that all conference participants can share. Whiteboard enables conference participants to collaborate on drawings and diagrams. To use Whiteboard, follow these steps:

1. Choose Tools⇨Whiteboard on the NetMeeting Menu bar (or press Ctrl+W) to open the Whiteboard window on each conference participant's screen.

2. To draw lines and shapes in the Whiteboard window, first click a drawing tool in the toolbar on the left side of the Whiteboard window. (You can choose from a pen, a highlight marker, outline or solid rectangles, or outline or solid ovals.) Then click a color in the color palette at the bottom of the Whiteboard window. Move the pointer into the drawing area (the large list box that occupies most of the Whiteboard window) and press and hold the mouse button as you drag the mouse.

If you draw lines with the pen or highlight marker tools, the lines appear along the path you drag until you release the mouse button. If you use a rectangle or oval tool, you define the size and position of the shape by starting in one corner and dragging to the opposite corner before releasing the mouse button.

3. To add text to a Whiteboard drawing, click the text tool in the toolbar (the big A) and then click a color in the color palette. Next, click in the drawing area where you want to position the text. When the flashing cursor appears, type the text with the keyboard.

4. To move or change an item already on the drawing area, click the selection tool in the toolbar (it looks like an arrow) and then click the shape or text with the selection tool. A dotted rectangle appears around the object to show that it's selected. You can drag the selected object with the selection tool to move it or you can click a color in the color palette to change the color of the object.

As you make changes in the drawing area of the Whiteboard window, NetMeeting replicates those changes on the other conference participants' screens. Likewise, any changes other participants make in the Whiteboard drawing appear in the Whiteboard window on your screen.

Sharing an application

You can share a program that is running on your computer and allow other NetMeeting users in conference with you to see and even use the program. (Application sharing can be very useful for demonstrations and can enable conference participants to collaborate on developing a document in a shared application window.) To use the Application Sharing feature, follow these steps:

1. Launch the application you want to share. The program must be running on your computer before you can share it.

2. Choose Tools⇨Share Application and then click the name of the program in the submenu that appears. NetMeeting opens a window for that program on each conference participant's screen.

Initially, you retain control of the shared program — other conference participants can observe but not control what happens in the program window.

3. To allow other conference participants to take control of the shared application, choose Tools⇨Start Collaborating. NetMeeting then allows other conference participants to take control of the shared program. They can scroll through the document in the shared application window, enter text, and make menu selections just as if they were using the mouse and keyboard on the machine on which the program is running.

Only one conference participant can control a shared application at any one time. When a remote user controls a shared application, the program ignores your input. Therefore, it can be dangerous to share Explorer windows and other programs that give access to your entire system.

4. To take control of an application being shared by another conference participant, double-click the shared program window.

5. To stop sharing a shared program, choose Tools⇨Share Application and then click the name of the program you want to stop sharing in the submenu that appears. NetMeeting closes the shared application window on the screens of the other participants, and they no longer can see the program.

Sending files

Along with everything else you can do in a NetMeeting conference, you can also send files to other conference participants. The easiest way to send files is to drag a file icon from a Windows Explorer or My Computer window and drop it on the list of conference participants in the NetMeeting window. NetMeeting sends the file to all the conference participants at once. You can also send a file by choosing Tools⇨File Transfer⇨Send File or pressing Ctrl+F.

Conversing via Microsoft Chat

Microsoft Chat is a chat program that enables you to conduct online, real-time conversations with other people — who are all disguised as weird cartoon characters. As a result, your conversations progress like panels of a cartoon strip, which can be mildly to hilariously entertaining.

To start Microsoft Chat and participate in a chat session, follow these steps:

1. Click the Start button on the Windows taskbar and then choose Programs⇨Microsoft Chat.

The Enter New Nickname dialog box appears in front of the Room – Microsoft Chat dialog box. Here, you enter the nickname (also known as a *handle*) that you want to be known by in the various chat rooms (my handle, for example, is Cyberdude).

2. Enter your handle in the Nickname text box and then click OK or press Enter.

After you choose a handle, the Connect dialog box appears so that you can get connected to one of the Comic Chat servers (the first time you start Microsoft Chat, the program automatically selects the initial Comic Chat server).

3. Click OK or press Enter in the Connect dialog box to connect to the Comic Chat server.

If you have trouble getting connected to the initial Comic Chat server, select one of the other servers in the Server drop-down list box or close the Connect dialog box and then the Room – Microsoft Chat window and try getting online at a later time.

After you get connected, Microsoft Chat displays the Comic_Chat – Microsoft Comic Chat window, which displays the panels of the dialog then in progress. The program also assigns you a cartoon character.

4. (Optional) To select a different cartoon character, choose View➪Options (or press Ctrl+Q) and then click a new character name in the Character list box on the Character tab.

As you click a new character name, the Preview area shows you how this character will look. To change the expression of the new character, drag the black dot to the desired facial expression on the circle below the character's preview image.

5. (Optional) To determine who else is currently in the Comic Chat room, scroll through the list of characters shown in the pane in the upper-right corner of the Chat window.

6. To participate in the chat session, type your comment or message in the text box in the pane at the bottom of the Chat window.

After typing your comment or message, you can post it publicly, either as something you're saying or something you're thinking.

7. To post your comment publicly to all the members in the chat room, click the Say button (or press Ctrl+Y) or the Think button (or press Ctrl+T) to the right of the text box.

To address something that you say to a particular member of the chat room, click on his or her character in the upper-right corner of the window before you click the Say button (or press Ctrl+Y). To post a message to just some of the members in the chat room, drag through their character names to select them in this panel in the upper-right corner before clicking the Whisper button (or pressing Ctrl+W).

8. To move to a different chat room, choose <u>R</u>oom⇨<u>R</u>oom List from the Chat menu bar and then double-click the name of the chat room in the Chat Room List dialog box.

9. After you finish chatting, click the Close button in the upper-right corner of the Chat window. To save your chat session so that you can review it or print it offline, choose <u>F</u>ile⇨<u>S</u>ave before closing the Chat window. The following figure shows you a chat session in full swing.

Microsoft Chat is so much fun that you can become addicted to it and its zany cartoon characters. Please don't get involved in any "comic" chats during business hours, because the continued use of Microsoft Chat could lead to your getting yourself fired!

Creating a Custom Web Page View for a Folder

When you choose <u>V</u>iew⇨as <u>W</u>eb Page and browse local disk drives and folders in any of the three browsing windows (My Computer, Windows Explorer, or Internet Explorer 4), Windows employs a default Web Page view. In this view, you see a bunch of vital statistics and thumbnail previews (when browsing graphics files or HTML documents) in the info panel on the left side of the pane displaying the folder's contents (*see* "Browsing folders with Web Page view turned on" in this part for more on this topic).

You can, if you want, customize a folder's default Web Page view by adding your own hyperlinks, text, or graphics images to the info panel. You can also customize the Web Page view by specifying a background graphic against which all the folder and file icons appear.

Customizing the info panel

To customize a folder's Web Page view by changing what information appears in the left info panel, follow these steps:

1. Open the folder for which you want to customize the Web Page view in one of the three browsing windows (My Computer, Windows Explorer, or Internet Explorer 4).

2. Choose View⇨Customize this folder to open the first dialog box of the Customize this folder wizard, which you see in the following figure.

3. To add your own text, graphics, and hyperlinks to the info panel that appears on the left, make sure that the Create or edit an HTML document radio button is selected and then click the Next button.

When you click the Next button with the Create or edit an HTML document radio button selected, a second dialog box of the Customize This Folder wizard appears. This second dialog box contains information on editing the hypertext template (named Folder.htt) with your HTML editor.

4. Choose the Next button to open the Folder.htt (hypertext template) that defines the folder's Web Page view in your HTML editor. (This editor is Windows Notepad if you don't have another HTML editor installed.)

When the Folder.htt document opens in an HTML editor like Notepad (which is really just a simple text editor), you see a bunch of (probably) indecipherable HTML tags and JavaScript programming (all surrounded by angle brackets).

The first thing you see is a comment (started by the ⟨!– tag and ended with the –⟩ tag) indicating this file was automatically generated using the Folder.htt hypertext template.

5. Use the Search function in your HTML editor (choose Search⟶Find if you are viewing the Folder.htt document in Notepad) to find the text a good place to add in the folder hypertext template.

Following the comment tag, ⟨!– HERE'S A GOOD PLACE TO ADD A FEW LINKS OF YOUR OWN –⟩, you see a couple of anchor tags with hyperlinks that have been commented out. You can use these hyperlinks by removing the ⟨! – (examples commented out) and –⟩ tags and editing the **mylink1.com** and **mylink2.com** part of the URL shown in the ⟨a href="http://www.mylink1.com"⟩ and the ⟨a href="http://www.mylink2.com"⟩ tags and replacing **the Custom Link 1** and **Custom Link 2** text that precedes the closing ⟨/a⟩ tags with descriptive text of your own.

6. Click the cursor at the place in the document where you want to add some stuff of your own, such as text or HTML tags to create hyperlinks to other Web pages (preferably by editing the commented out anchors as indicated in the preceding step) or to display JPEG or GIF graphic images.

For help on entering HTML tags, you might want to get your hands on a copy of *HTML For Dummies,* by Ed Tittel and Steve James, or *HTML For Dummies Quick Reference,* by Eric and Deborah Ray (both published by IDG Books Worldwide, Inc.).

7. Click the Close box in the HTML editor's window and then click Yes when asked to save your changes to the Folder.htt document.

As soon as you close the HTML editor after saving your changes, the last dialog box of the Customize this Folder wizard appears, congratulating you for making changes to the Folder.htt hypertext template file.

8. Click the Finish button in the final dialog box of the Customize this Folder wizard to close the wizard and put your changes into effect.

As soon as you close the Customize this Folder wizard, you are returned to the browsing window from where you launched the wizard when you chose View⟶Customize this Folder. There, you will see the effects of the changes you made to the info panel. Note that Windows automatically turns on the Web Page view for the folder even if the View⟶as Web Page command was not originally selected at the time you chose View⟶Customize this Folder.

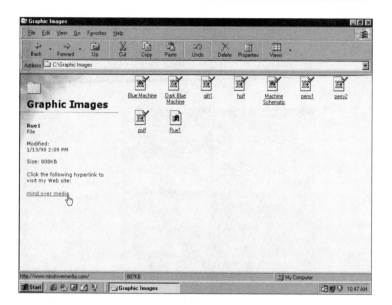

 The customized Folder.htt file that defines your folder's Web Page view and resides in the folder is not displayed in any of the three browsing windows unless the Show All Files radio button on the View tab of the Folder Options dialog box is selected when you display the folder's contents. (*See* "Changing the View options" in this part for details.)

Adding a background graphic to the Web Page view

In addition to (or instead of) customizing the contents of the info panel, you can customize a folder's Web Page view by adding a background graphic image.

To add a background graphic against which the folder's icons appear, follow these steps:

1. Open the folder for which you want to add a background graphic image in one of the three browsing windows (My Computer, Windows Explorer, or Internet Explorer 4).

2. Choose View➪Customize this folder to open the first dialog box of the Customize this Folder wizard.

3. Select the Choose a background picture radio button and then click the Next button.

When you click the Next button with the Choose a background graphic radio button selected, a second dialog box of the Customize this Folder wizard appears, where you can select the graphic image to use or you can change the color of the caption text that appears with the folder's icons.

4. Click the name of the background graphic you want to use in the Background picture for this folder list box (a preview of the graphic then appears in the tall list box on the left). If the graphic you want to use is in another folder, click the Browse button and then select the folder containing the image in the Open dialog box, and then click the Open button.

5. (Optional) To change the color of the caption text that accompanies the folder icons (the default is black), click the button with the color sample to the right of Text and choose a new color from the pop-up color palette. If you want to add a background color against which the caption text appears, click the check box in front of the dimmed Background option to activate it and then click the button with the color sample to its right and choose a color from its pop-up color palette.

6. Click the Next button to advance to the Congratulations dialog box of the Customize this Folder wizard, where the name of the graphic file you selected appears.

7. Click the Finish button to close the Customize this Folder wizard and return to the folder in the browsing window from which you launched the wizard.

When you return to the browsing window, the folder's icons in the main part now appear against the fancy new graphic image you just selected.

Be careful when selecting a background graphic, because almost any image heavier than the Clouds.bmp makes it difficult, if not impossible, to read the folder icons (especially if you don't change the text caption color and the image uses dark colors).

Also, be aware that any background graphic that you add to a folder remains displayed even when you turn off the Web Page view! The only way to get rid of an offending image is to remove the customization to the Web Page view, as described in the following section (which not only gets rid of the graphic but also removes any changes you made to the info panel).

Removing a customized Web Page view

You can remove any and all customization to a folder's Web Page view by following these few steps:

1. Open the folder for which you want to add a background graphic image in one of the three browsing windows (My Computer, Windows Explorer, or Internet Explorer 4).

2. Choose View⇨Customize this Folder to open the first dialog box of the Customize this Folder wizard.

3. Select the Remove customization radio button and then click the Next button to advance to the next dialog box, where you are informed that the Folder.htt file will be moved to the Recycle Bin and that settings stored in the Windows Desktop.ini file will be removed.

4. Click the Next button to advance to the Congratulations dialog box of the Customize this Folder wizard and then click the Finish button to close the Customize this Folder wizard, remove all the customized settings, and return to the folder in the browsing window from which you launched the wizard.

When you return to the browsing window, the graphic used as the folder's background disappears, as will all your changes to the info panel.

Searching the Web

The World Wide Web holds an enormous wealth of information on almost every subject known to humanity — and it is of absolutely no use if you don't know how to get to it. To help Web surfers like yourself locate the sites containing the information you need, a number of so-called *search engines* have been designed. Each search engine maintains a slightly different directory of the sites on the World Wide Web (which are mostly maintained and updated by automated programs called by such wonderfully suggestive names as Web crawlers, spiders, and robots!).

Searching from the Explorer bar

The three browsing windows (My Computer, Windows Explorer, and Internet Explorer 4) give you access to all the most popular search engines through the Explorer bar. You can open the Search Explorer bar in one of two ways:

+ Choose View⇨Explorer Bar⇨Search.

+ Click the Search button on the Standard Buttons toolbar. (Note that this button does not appear on this toolbar when you browse local folders.)

After you open the Search Explorer bar, Windows randomly picks one of the search engines as its Pick-of-the-day. For example, the last time I opened the Search Explorer bar, Internet Explorer chose the Excite search engine as the Pick-of-the-day.

If you want, you can go ahead and use the search engine featured as the Pick-of-the-day, or you can select a new engine from the Select Provider drop-down list box.

After you select your search engine, you are ready to enter the word or words (known affectionately as a *search string* in programmers parlance) that you want the engine to search for in the Web sites listed in its directory.

To avoid getting back thousands and thousands of irrelevant search results (or, at the very minimum, uninteresting ones), you often need to consider whether you want the search engine to returns links only to sites that contain all the terms you enter in the search string. Suppose that I want to find sites that deal with Thai cuisine. If I enter the search string

```
Thai cuisine
```

in the Excite search string text box, the search engine will return not only links to Web sites that have "Thai" in their descriptions (like all the travel sites that deal with Thailand — without any reference to their style of cooking), but also links to all sites that have "cuisine" (regardless of what type) in their descriptions. The problem with this approach is that it can give you far too many extraneous results.

With many search engines, this result occurs because they search for each term in the search string *independently* as well as *together* when you enter it in the search string text box (as though I had asked for Web sites whose descriptions contain "Thai" and/or "cuisine").

TIP

The easiest way to tell a search engine that you want links to a Web site returned only when *all* the terms in your search string are matched in their descriptions is to enclose all the terms in double quotation marks. So, in the case of the Thai cuisine search string, to find more Web sites that deal only with this particular type of cooking, I would enter

```
"Thai cuisine"
```

in the search string text box. Taking this little extra step can often give fewer results — but results that are also much more to your liking.

When you click the Search button (or its equivalent, which can be called something gross like "Go Get It") or press Enter to have the search engine begin searching its directory, Windows often interrupts you with its Security Alert dialog box. This dialog box begins by giving you the earth-shattering news that you are about to send information over the Internet. It then goes on to tell you that it may be possible for other people to see what you are sending. Because you are doing nothing more dangerous than searching the directory of a search engine, you can go ahead and click the Yes button in response to the question Do you want to continue? to process the search.

When the search engine finishes processing your search string, it returns a list of hyperlinks in the Search Explorer bar, which represent the top ten matches. You can then click any of the hyperlinks in the list to display that Web page in the area of the browsing window to the right of the Explorer bar.

If you want, you can add the Web page to your Favorites (*see* "Adding to Your Favorites" earlier in this part for details) so that you can return to it without repeating the search. If you aren't interested, you can try another of the hyperlinks in the Explorer bar to see if its Web page is of more interest.

Note that at anytime during the process of checking out the matches to your search, you can temporarily remove the Search Explorer bar so that Web page's contents are displayed in a full-screen: Just click the Search button on the Standard Buttons bar. Then, if you decide after browsing the page's contents that you want to check out another of the pages in the results list, you can restore the Search Explorer bar by clicking the Search button again.

After exhausting the links in the top ten list, you can display links to the next ten matching pages returned by the search engine by clicking some sort of Next button (in the case of the Excite search engine, this button appears with the text `Next 11-20` on it).

After you are convinced that you've seen the best matches to your search, you can conduct another search with the same search engine using slightly different terms, or you can switch to another search engine to see what kinds of results it produces using the same search string.

Autosearching from the Address bar

In addition to searching from the Search Explorer bar, Windows enables you to perform searches from the Address bar, using a feature referred to as Autosearching. To conduct an Autosearch from the Address bar, you need to click the Address bar to select its current entry and then preface the search string with one of the following three terms:

- ✦ Go
- ✦ Find
- ✦ ?

To search for Web sites whose descriptions contain the terms *Thai cuisine,* for example, you could type

`go Thai cuisine`

or

`find Thai cuisine`

or even

`? Thai cuisine`

in the Address bar. After you enter **go**, **find**, or **?** followed by the search string, press the Enter key to have Windows conduct the search.

Note that, unlike when conducting a search from the Explorer window, when you follow one of the hyperlinks returned as a match, the Web page referenced by the link entirely replaces the page with the list of search results. The result is that you have to use the Back button or its keyboard equivalent (press Alt+←) to return to the page of search results in order to follow another of its links.

If you want to search for matches to your original search string, scroll down the Web page with the search results until you see the Search Yahoo! button. Then click this button to continue to search with the Yahoo! search engine, using the same search string.

Doing an all-in-one search

If you don't mind searching from a single screen of information, the three browsing windows (My Computer, Windows Explorer, and Internet Explorer 4) offer you yet a third method for searching the Web.

When you choose Go⊅Search the Web, Windows goes online and opens a Search page on the Microsoft Home Web site, as shown in the following figure. The top pane of the Search page offers you a choice of five different search engines (Lycos, Excite, Yahoo, Infoseek, or AOL NetFind), and the bottom pane offers you a choice of more search engines (such as AltaVista, HotBot, and WebCrawler) and other specialized online directories and guides.

To conduct a search, click the radio button for the search engine, directory, or guide that you want to use and then enter the word or words you want to search for before pressing Enter to start the search.

 Keep in mind when using the Search page that you must use the Back and Forward buttons to go back and forth between the matching pages that you visit and to get back to the Search page to conduct another search or to see the next group of 10 matches. (That is the reason I far-and-away prefer using the Search Explorer bar to do my Web searches.)

Sending and Receiving E-Mail with Outlook Express

Outlook Express is the name of the e-mail software that is installed with Windows 98. You can use this program to compose, send, and read e-mail messages and to subscribe to the newsgroups supported by your Internet service provider, which enables you to read the newsgroup's messages as well as respond to them.

Composing and sending a new e-mail message

To compose and send a new e-mail message in Outlook Express, follow these steps:

1. In one of the three browsing windows (My Computer, Windows Explorer, or Internet Explorer 4), choose Go⇨Mail or click the Launch Outlook Express button on the Quick Launch toolbar on the Windows taskbar.

If you use the Go⇨Mail command, the Outlook Express window opens with the Outlook Express icon selected in the left pane and general information displayed in the right pane. If you use the Launch Outlook Express button, the window opens with the Inbox icon selected in the left pane and the contents of the inbox shown in two panes, one on top of the other, on the right.

2. Click the Compose Message button at the beginning of the Outlook Express toolbar or choose Compose⇨New Message (or press Ctrl+N) to open a New Message window.

The first thing to do in a new message is to specify the recipient's e-mail address in the To: field (which automatically contains the cursor). You can either type this address in the To: text box or you can click the Select recipients from a list button that appears to the immediate left of the cursor if you want to select the e-mail address from your Windows Address Book or one of the online directories.

3. Type the recipient's e-mail address in the text box of the To: field or, if the recipient is listed in your Windows Address Book, click the Select recipients from a list button to open the Select Recipients dialog box. Then you click the name of the recipient in the Name list box before you click the To:-> button followed by the OK button.

When composing a new message, you can send copies of it to as many other recipients (within reason) that you want. To send copies of the message to other recipients, you enter their e-mail addresses in the Cc: field (if you don't care if they see all of the other people copied on the message) or in the Bcc: field (if you don't want them to see any of the other people copied on the message).

4. (Optional) Click somewhere in the <click here to enter carbon copy recipients> text in the Cc: field or somewhere in the <click here to enter blind carbon copy recipients> and then type their e-mail addresses, separated by semicolons (;), in the Cc: or Bcc: fields. Alternatively, if their addresses are entered in the Windows Address Book, click the Select recipients from a list button to open the Select Recipients dialog box and then choose their e-mail addresses there (after clicking the names in the Name list box, click the C̲c-> button to add them to the copy list or click the B̲cc-> to add them to the blind copy list).

After filling in the e-mail addresses of the recipients, you are ready to enter the subject of the message. The descriptive text that you enter in the Subject: field of the message appears in the upper pane of the recipients' Inbox when they read the message.

5. Click somewhere in the `<click here to enter the subject>` text in the Subject: field and then enter a brief description of the contents or purpose of the e-mail message.

In Outlook Express, you can change the priority of the e-mail message from normal to either high or low. When you make a message either high or low priority, Outlook Express attaches a priority icon to the message (assuming that the recipients of the message are using Outlook Express to read their mail) that indicates its relative importance. The high-priority icon has an exclamation mark in front of the envelope, whereas the low-priority icon has an arrow pointing downward.

6. (Optional) To boost the priority of the message, choose T̲ools⇨Set P̲riority and then choose H̲igh in the submenu that appears. To decrease the priority of the message, click the Priority button and choose L̲ow on the submenu.

When you select H̲igh priority, the Internet Explorer icon in the picture of the stamp in the Priority button is replaced with a red exclamation point. When you select L̲ow Priority, it is replaced with a blue arrow pointing down.

7. Click the cursor in the body of the message and then type in the text of the message as you would in any text editor or word processor, ending paragraphs and short lines by pressing the Enter key.

As soon as you click the cursor in the body of the message, the formatting toolbar that separates the header section of the message from the body window becomes activated. You can then use its buttons to format the text of the message, as shown in the following figure.

When composing the text of the message, keep in mind that you can insert text directly into the body of the message from other documents via the Clipboard (the old Cut, Copy, and Paste commands) or, in the case of text or an HTML document, by choosing I̲nsert⇨T̲ext from File.

Font   Font Size   Underline   Align Center

Send   Style tag   Italic   Font Color
Message
button   Bold   Align Left   Align Right

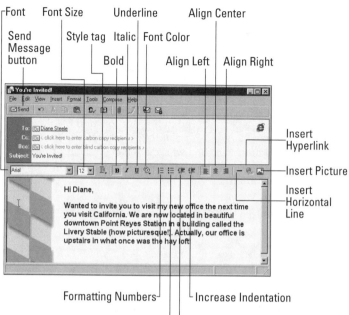

Insert
Hyperlink

Insert Picture

Insert
Horizontal
Line

Formatting Numbers   Increase Indentation
Formatting Bullets   Decrease Indentation

8. (Optional) If you're not sure of some (or all) of the spelling in the text of the body of the message, you can have Outlook Express check the spelling by inserting the cursor at the beginning of the message text and then choosing Tools⇨Spelling, or by pressing F7.

When spell-checking the message, Outlook Express flags each word that it cannot find in the dictionary and tries its best to suggest an alternate word.

To replace the unknown word in the text with the word suggested in the Change To text box of the Spelling window, click the Change button, or, if it's a word that occurs frequently in the rest of the text, click Change All.

To ignore the unknown word and have the spelling checker continue to scan the rest of the text for possible misspellings, click Ignore, or, if it's a word that occurs frequently in the rest of the text, click Ignore All.

9. (Optional) To send a file along with your e-mail message, choose Insert⇨File Attachment and then select the file in the Insert Attachment dialog box and click the Attach button.

When you include a file with a message, an icon for the file appears in a new horizontal pane at the bottom of the body of the e-mail message.

10. To send the e-mail message to its recipients, click the Send
Message button on the Outlook Express toolbar or press
Ctrl+Enter or Alt+S.

If you compose e-mail messages when you cannot get online to
send them, choose File⇨Send Later from the New Message
window's menu bar after you finish composing each message.
Outlook Express then displays an alert box indicating that the
message will be stored in the Outbox, and it will be sent the next
time you click the Send and Receive button. To send the messages
stored in the Outbox when you can connect or are connected to
the Internet, just click the Send and Receive button on the Outlook
Express toolbar.

Adding a recipient to your Windows Address Book

Outlook Express makes it easy to maintain an address book
(called the Windows Address Book), where you can store the
e-mail addresses for all the people you regularly correspond with.
If you are switching from some other e-mail program (like the one
that comes with Netscape Navigator) and you have created an
address book with that program, you can even import all of its
addresses into the Windows Address Book, making it unnecessary
to reenter them.

To add a new recipient to the Windows Address Book, follow these
steps:

1. Open Outlook Express by clicking the Launch the Outlook
Express button on the Quick Launch toolbar or by choosing
Go⇨Mail in one of the three browsing windows (My Com-
puter, Windows Explorer, or Internet Explorer 4).

2. Click the Address Book button on the Outlook Express toolbar,
or press Ctrl+Shift+B, to open the Windows Address Book, as
shown in the following figure.

3. Click the New Contact button at the beginning of the Windows Address Book toolbar or choose File➪New Contact to open the Properties dialog box, which opens with the Personal tab selected.

Note that you can also open the Properties dialog box by clicking the New Contact button in the Select Recipients dialog box, which you open by clicking the Select Recipients from a List button in the To:, Cc:, or Bcc: fields of the message header.

4. Fill in the Name information for the new contact in the various name fields and then select the Add new text box in the E-Mail Addresses section, where you type the recipient's e-mail address before clicking the Add button.

When you click the Add button, Outlook Express adds the e-mail address you enter into the list box, automatically designating it as the Default E-Mail.

If the person you are adding to the Windows Address Book has more than one e-mail address (as would be the case if he or she maintains an e-mail account at home with one address and an e-mail account at work with another address), you can add the additional e-mail address.

5. (Optional) Repeat Step 4 to add an additional e-mail address for the same recipient.

If you want to make the second e-mail address the default address that Outlook Express automatically uses when you compose a new message, you need to select the second address in the list box and then click the Set as Default button.

TIP

To use a contact's alternate e-mail address in a new message, you need to select the person's name in the Select Recipients dialog box and then click the Properties button, where you make the alternate e-mail address the new default with the Set as Default button.

6. Click the OK button to close the Properties dialog box and return to the Windows Address Book window, where the contact's name appears, followed by the new default e-mail address.

7. Click the Close button in the upper-right corner of the Windows Address Book window to close it.

To import the addresses from an address book created with Eudora, Microsoft Exchange, Microsoft Internet Mail for Windows, Netscape Navigator, or stored in a comma-separated text file into the Windows Address Book, use these steps:

1. Open the Windows Address Book window as described in Steps 1 and 2 of the preceding procedure for adding a new contact.

2. Choose File⇨Import⇨Address Book from the Windows Address Book menu bar to open the Windows Address Book Import Tool dialog box.

3. Click the type of address book you want to import in the list box of the Windows Address Book Import Tool dialog box. Then click the Import button.

After Outlook Express imports the names and e-mail addresses of all the contacts in the existing address book, it closes the Windows Address Book Import Tool dialog box and returns you to the Windows Address Book dialog box. The imported contacts now appear in that dialog box.

4. (Optional) To sort the contacts in the Windows Address Book by last names, click the Names button at the top of the first entry. To sort the contacts by e-mail addresses, click the E-mail Address button instead.

5. Click the Close button in the upper-right corner of the Windows Address Book window to close it.

Reading and responding to your e-mail

When you use Outlook Express as your e-mail program, you read the messages that you receive in an area known as the Inbox. To open the Inbox in Outlook Express and read your e-mail messages, take these steps:

1. Open the Inbox in Outlook Express either by choosing Go⇨Mail on the menu bar of one of the three browsing windows (My Computer, Windows Explorer, or Internet Explorer 4) or by clicking the Launch Outlook Express button on the Quick Launch toolbar on the taskbar *and* then clicking the Inbox icon in the pane on the left.

When browsing Web pages in one of the three browsing windows, you can also open the Inbox in Outlook Express by clicking the Mail button on the Standard Buttons bar and then choosing Read Mail on the pop-up menu that appears.

Send and Receive

2. Click the Send and Receive button on the Outlook Express toolbar, or press Ctrl+M, to have Outlook Express check your Mail server and download any new messages.

As soon as you click the Send and Receive button, Outlook Express opens a connection to your Mail server, where it checks for any new messages to download. New messages are then downloaded to your computer.

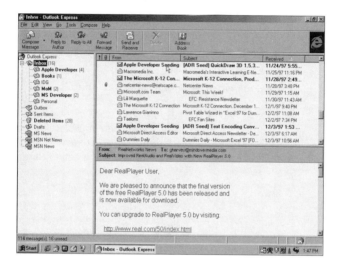

Descriptions of any new messages appear in bold at the bottom of the list in the upper pane of the Inbox, which is divided into five columns: Priority (indicated by the red exclamation point), Attachments (indicated by the paper clip), From, Subject, and Received (showing both the date and time that the e-mail message was downloaded on your computer).

Note that mail messages that you haven't yet read are not only indicated by bold type but also by a sealed envelope icon in the From column. Mail messages that you *have* read are indicated by an opened envelope icon.

3. To read one of your new messages, click any column of its description in the upper pane of the Inbox.

The text of the message you select appears in the lower pane of the Inbox, and the From and Subject information appears on the bar dividing the upper pane from the lower. If the message has one or more files attached to it, a paper clip appears on the right side of this bar.

4. (Optional) To open the file or files attached to the e-mail message with its native program (or, at least, one that can open the file), click the paper clip icon and then click the button containing the name of the file that pops up from the paper clip.

Sometimes, you may need to get a hard copy of the message to share with other, less fortunate workers in the office who don't have e-mail. (If they do have e-mail, forward the message to them instead, as covered in optional Step 8.)

5. (Optional) To print the contents of an e-mail message, choose File⇨Print, or press Ctrl+P, and then click OK in the Print dialog box.

Occasionally, an e-mail message will contain some information that you want to be able to reuse in other documents without having to retype it. Rather than having to open the message in the Outlook Express Inbox and then copy its contents to a new document via the Clipboard, you can save it as either a text file or an HTML file (both of which can be opened in a word processor like Word 97).

6. (Optional) To save the contents of an e-mail message as a text file or an HTML file, choose File⇨Save As to open the Save Message As dialog box. Next, choose the folder in which to save the file in the Save in drop-down list box, and the file format in which to save the file in the Save as type drop-down list box. Then click the Save button.

If the e-mail message uses the High Priority (!) icon, chances are good that you may have to reply to it right away. You can respond to the message either by clicking the Reply to Author or the Reply to All button.

After you click one of these buttons, Outlook Express opens a message window in which:

- The sender of the original message is listed as the recipient in the To: field.

- The subject of the original message appear in the Subject: field, followed by the term Re: (regarding).

- The contents of the original message appear in the body of the reply beneath the heading, `– Original Message–` , followed by the From:, To:, Date:, and Subject: information from the original message.

7. (Optional) To reply to the author of the e-mail message, click the Reply to Author button on the Outlook Express toolbar. To send copies of the reply to all the others copied on the original message as well, click the Reply to All button instead. Then add the text of your reply above the text of the original message and send the reply (by pressing Ctrl+Enter or Alt+S).

Sometimes, in addition to or instead of replying to the original message, you need to send a copy of it to someone who was not listed in the Cc: field. To send a copy to this person, you forward a copy of the original message to the new recipients of your choosing. When you forward a message, Outlook Express copies the Subject: and contents of the original message to a new message, which you then address and send.

8. (Optional) To forward the e-mail message to another e-mail address, click the Forward Message button on the Outlook Express toolbar. Then fill in the recipient information in the To:, and, if applicable, Cc: and Bcc fields, add any additional text of your own above that of the original message, and send the forwarded message on its way (by pressing Ctrl+Enter or Alt+S).

9. After you read and respond to your e-mail, click the Close box in the upper-right corner of the Outlook Express Inbox window.

Setting Outlook Express to check for mail automatically

Normally, when you launch Outlook Express, the program does not automatically inform you when you have new e-mail except when you specifically click the Send and Receive button on the toolbar. If you want, you can have Outlook Express automatically inform you of new e-mail anytime you open the program. To set up this capability, follow these steps:

1. Open Outlook Express by clicking the Launch the Outlook Express button on the Quick Launch toolbar or by choosing Go⇨Mail in one of the three browsing windows (My Computer, Windows Explorer, or Internet Explorer 4).

2. Choose Tools⇨Options from the Outlook Express menu bar to open the Options dialog box, which appears with the General tab selected.

3. Choose the Check for new messages every 30 minutes check box to put a check mark in it and then replace 30 in the associated text box with any new desired number of minutes, or use the spinner buttons to select this interval value.

When you enable the Check for new messages every "so many" minutes check box, Outlook Express automatically checks your mail server for new messages whenever you launch the program and then continues to check at the specified interval as you work in the program.

4. (Optional) To have Outlook Express play a chime whenever new e-mail messages are downloaded while you're working in the program, choose the Play sound when new messages arrive check box.

5. Click OK to close the Options dialog box and return to Outlook Express and put into effect the automatic checking for e-mail.

After the automatic e-mail checking goes into effect, Outlook Express informs you of the delivery of new e-mail by placing an envelope icon on the Outlook Express Status bar (and "dinging" if you enabled Play sound when new messages arrive check box).

Organizing your e-mail

Getting e-mail is great, but it doesn't take long for you to end up with a disorganized mess. If you are anything like me, your Outlook Express Inbox will end up with hundreds of messages, some of which are still unread — and all of which are lumped together in one extensive list.

Outlook Express makes it easy to arrange your e-mail messages in folders. To send a bunch of related e-mail messages into a new or existing folder, you follow these steps:

1. Open the Inbox in Outlook Express either by choosing Go➪Mail on the menu bar of one of the three browsing windows (My Computer, Windows Explorer, or Internet Explorer 4) or by clicking the Launch Outlook Express button on the Quick Launch toolbar on the taskbar *and* then clicking the Inbox icon in the pane on the left.

2. Select all the messages that you want to put in the same folder. To select a single message, click its description. To select a continuous series of messages, click the first one and hold down the Shift key as you click the last one. To click multiple messages that aren't in a series, hold down Ctrl as you click the description of each one.

3. After you select the messages to be moved, choose Edit➪Move To Folder on the Outlook Express menu bar to open the Move dialog box.

4. Click the Inbox folder icon and then click the name of the subfolder into which the selected messages are to be moved, as you see in the following figure. If you need to create a new folder for the selected items, click the <u>N</u>ew Folder button, enter the name in the <u>F</u>older Name text box, and click OK. Then click the Inbox folder icon before clicking the name of the newly created subfolder.

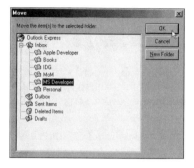

5. Click the OK button in the Move dialog box to move the messages into the selected folder.

To verify that the items are now in the correct folder, click the folder's icon in the outline (beneath the Inbox icon) that appears in the left pane of the Outlook Express window.

Don't forget that the most basic way to organize your e-mail is by sorting all the messages in the Inbox (or any of the other Outlook Express folders, for that matter) by clicking its column button. For example, if you want to sort the e-mail in your Inbox by subject, you click the Subject button at the top of list. So, too, if you want to sort the messages by the date and time received (from earliest to most recent), you click the Received button at the top of that column.

Deleting and compacting your e-mail

As you get more and more e-mail in your Inbox, you will want to use the <u>F</u>ile⇨<u>F</u>older⇨C<u>o</u>mpact command to compress the messages, thus freeing up valuable disk space. When you have e-mail in all sorts of different folders, you can compact all the messages by choosing <u>F</u>ile⇨<u>F</u>older⇨Compact <u>A</u>ll Folders instead.

When you have messages (especially those unsolicited ones) that you no longer need to store on your computer's hard drive, you can get rid of the messages permanently by selecting them and then choosing <u>E</u>dit⇨<u>D</u>elete (press Ctrl+D). Then you choose <u>Y</u>es in the alert box telling you that you are about to delete forever the selected messages.

To remove messages from the Inbox without permanently getting rid of them, select them and then press the Delete key. They instantly disappear from the Inbox window. If you ever need them again, however, you can display them by clicking the Deleted Items icon in the pane on the left side of the Outlook Express window.

To get rid of all the items in the Deleted Items folder, right-click its icon in the left pane of the Outlook Express window and then choose the Empty Folder command on the icon's shortcut menu.

Setting Up the Channel Screen Saver

Many of the Web channels that you subscribe to contain a component for adding the channel's home page to a special Channel Screen Saver, which ships as one of your screen saver choices in Windows 98.

To activate the Channel Screen Saver and customize which channels appear in its slide show, you follow these steps:

1. In the Windows desktop, right-click somewhere on the desktop and then choose the Properties command from the desktop's shortcut menu. Or you can click the Start button on the taskbar and then choose Settings➪Active Desktop➪ Customize my Desktop to open the Display Properties dialog box.

2. Click the Screen Saver tab in the Display Properties dialog box.

3. Choose the Channel Screen Saver selection in the Screen Saver drop-down list box.

4. Click the Settings button to open the Screen Saver Properties dialog box, as shown in the following figure.

When the Screen Saver Properties dialog box opens, its Channels list box shows all the Web channels to which you've subscribed that offer a screen-saver version.

5. To include a channel in the Channel Screen Saver slide show, click the check box preceding its name in the Channels list box. To remove a channel that you no longer want to appear as part of the Channel Screen Saver's slide show, click its check box to remove the check mark.

By default, the Channel Screen Saver displays the home page of each channel you select in the Channels list box a total of 30 seconds before displaying the home page of the next one in the list.

6. (Optional) To change the amount of time that the opening screen of each channel in the screen saver is displayed, enter a new value in the Display each Channel for text box or use the spinner buttons to select the new value.

7. (Optional) To disable any sound effects that the opening channel page uses, click the Play background sounds check box to remove its check mark.

Normally, a screen saver stops only when you click the Close button that appears in the upper-right corner of the screen after you move the mouse. If you prefer, you can have the screen saver stop running as soon as you press any key or move the mouse. Note, however, that when you close the Channel Screen Saver by moving the mouse, you have no way of interacting with the Channel page, because it is impossible to click any of the page's hyperlinks or buttons without first moving the mouse and thereby closing the screen saver.

8. (Optional) To close the Channel Screen Saver and return to the desktop or active application by moving the mouse, click the Close the Screen Saver by moving the mouse radio button.

9. Click OK to close the Screen Saver Properties dialog box and return to the Display Properties dialog box.

10. (Optional) To preview the Channel Screen Saver, click the Preview button.

11. Click OK to close the Display Properties dialog box.

Subscribing to Channels

Active Channels (also known simply as channels) are Web sites that make use of a fairly new technology called *Webcasting,* which enables Internet Explorer 4.0 automatically to download updated contents from the Channel Web site to your computer cache on a regular schedule.

To have Windows monitor an Active Channel Web site and automatically download its updated content, you need to "subscribe" to the channel, a process in which you set up when and how the automatic downloading is to take place.

Channel subscriptions offer you several significant benefits over normal Web browsing:

✦ The Internet Explorer browser in Windows automatically monitors the channel for changes to its contents, so you don't need to keep returning to the Web site to get its updated files.

✦ Updated channel contents are normally automatically downloaded to your computer's cache during nonbusiness hours (while you're fast asleep in your little bed), so you don't have to face the terrible Internet traffic gridlock that makes the World Wide Wait so annoying — just to stay on top of the latest information from regularly changing sites (like News and online magazine channels).

✦ You can browse updated channel content offline, enabling you to view the new information even when you cannot be connected to the Internet, such as when you're in transit on a plane or bus (*see* "Browsing Web pages offline" in this part for details).

✦ Even for those times when you need to manually update a channel's contents during regular business hours, channels make it easier to get connected, because you can use the Channel bar without any reference to the Web site's URL (the http://, www, .com thingy).

✦ The Channel bar in the Active Channel Viewer (a special display view of the Internet Explorer) that you use to browse channel contents (*see* "Viewing Active Channels" in this part) offers you the familiar outline view of all the pages in a channel, making it easy to get to and display just the pages that you're interested in.

✦ Many channels offer a more "condensed" experience of their information than traditional Web sites, giving you immediate access to the information you want to see without having to browse through Web page after Web page. In their most concentrated form, some channels even enable you to place a compressed form of their channel contents directly on your Windows desktop as an Active Desktop item (*see* "Adding Active Desktop Items" earlier in this part for details), giving you instant access to highlights or headlines from the Web site, which, when clicked, open into full-screen Web pages.

Using the Channel Guide to subscribe to a channel

The procedure for subscribing to a channel is a breeze, thanks to a little thing developed by Microsoft called the Microsoft Channel Guide. The Microsoft Channel Guide enables you to preview and, if you like what you see, subscribe to a variety of channels. The channels in the channel guide fall into the following categories:

- ✦ News & Technology
- ✦ Sports
- ✦ Business
- ✦ Entertainment
- ✦ Lifestyle & Travel

Note that, for now, it costs nothing to subscribe to most of the channels out there in cyberspace (they don't yet operate like premium channels on cable TV). That is not to say, however, that you won't find some channels charging for their content or, at least, for some sections of the channel site.

Subscribing to channels via the Microsoft Channel Guide

You can open the Microsoft Channel Guide directly from the Windows desktop or from within any of the three browsing windows (My Computer, Windows Explorer, and Internet Explorer 4).

To open the channel guide from the Windows desktop, use one of these methods:

- ✦ Click the Microsoft Channel Guide button on the Internet Explorer Channel Bar (assuming that the Web Page view for the desktop is turned on — *see* "Activating/Deactivating the Active Desktop" earlier in this part for details).

- ✦ Click the View Channels button on the Quick Launch toolbar on the Windows taskbar and then click the Channel Guide button at the top of the sliding Channel Explorer bar.

To open the Microsoft Channel Guide from within one of the three browsing windows (My Computer, Windows Explore, or Internet Explorer 4), use one of these methods:

✦ Choose F̲avorites⇨Channels⇨Channel Guide from the window's menu bar.

✦ Choose V̲iew⇨E̲xplorer Bar⇨C̲hannels and then click the Channel Guide button at the top of the Channel Explorer bar. You can also open the Channel Explorer bar by clicking the Channels button on the Standard Buttons bar when browsing Web pages.

When you click the Channel Guide button, the Active Channel Guide Welcome page opens, displaying tabs for each of the channel categories, as shown in the following figure. Beneath the category tab is a description and the button for one of the channels in that category. (If you wait long enough, you will see these descriptions and buttons change as the page cycles through the channels listed in each of the categories.)

To preview the channels in a particular category, click the category tab of interest. To preview the particular channel currently displayed beneath one of the category tabs, click its channel button.

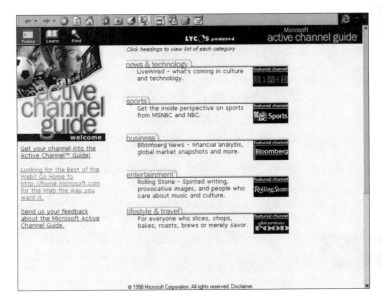

When you click a category tab, Windows uses the Lycos search engine to locate all the channels in that category. The program then displays for the selected category a Web page that is divided into three parts:

+ In the center area beneath the name of the category, the page displays a text box and buttons that you can use to search for particular channels in the category (*see* "Searching for channels" in this part for details).

+ In a column to the left of the Find feature information, the page displays the buttons for the first seven channels in this category. (The ranking of the channels in any given category is random and is therefore subject to change each time you preview the channels in that category.) To display the buttons for the next seven channels in the category, click the Next 7 button at the bottom of this column. (You can redisplay the first group by clicking the Previous 7 button that then appears at the top of the column of channel buttons.) Note that some of the channels near the end of a category display hyperlinks rather than buttons.

+ To the left of the column with the buttons for the first seven channels in the category, you see the total number of channels in the category, followed by hyperlinks that divide the total number of channels into groups of seven. When you click one of these hyperlinks, Internet Explorer 4 displays the buttons for the channels in that group.

To return to the Welcome page of the Active Channel Guide, where you can select another channel category, click the Today button that appears at the far left of the title bar (immediately above the statistic indicating the total number of channels in the category). To get general information about channels, click the Learn button (to the immediate right of the Today button on the title bar).

As you pass the mouse pointer over the channel buttons displayed in the category's channel guide page, the Find information in the center of the Web page is replaced by a description of the channel. As soon as you click one of the channel buttons or hyperlinks to a channel, the information describing the channel is replaced by a full-fledged preview of the channel. If you then decide that you want to subscribe to the channel whose preview is being displayed, you can do so by following these steps:

1. Click the Add Active Channel button in the preview of the channel.

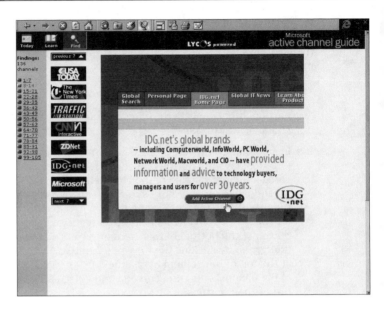

Note that some channels contain an Add to Active Desktop button in addition to the Add Active Channel button. If you click the Add to Active Desktop, Windows adds a special desktop-item version of the channel to the Windows desktop (*see* "Adding Active Desktop Items" earlier in this part for details).

This dialog box enables you to select how you are to be informed of updates to the channel, edit the descriptive name of the channel, and decide in which folder to create the channel (which, in turn, decides where the channel's button appears on the Internet Explorer Channel bar on the desktop and the Channel Explorer bar).

By default, the Add Active Channel (TM) content dialog box selects the Yes, notify me of updates and download the channel for offline viewing radio button.

2. (Optional) If you want to subscribe to the channel but don't want to have its content automatically downloaded, choose the Yes, but only tell me when updates occur radio button. If you want to add the channel's button to Channel Explorer bar without subscribing to its content (so that you can revisit the Web site by merely clicking the channel button), choose the No, just add it to my channel bar radio button.

3. (Optional) To change the descriptive name of the channel (as it appears on the Explorer Channel bar), edit the default channel name in the Name text box.

4. (Optional) To add the channel to one of the category folders (Business, Entertainment, Lifestyle and Travel, News and Technology, or Sports), click the Create in button to expand the Add Active Channel(TM) content dialog box. This action displays the Channels folder and all of its category subfolders in the Create In list box. Then select the subfolder in which you want the new channel added by clicking it.

5. Click OK to complete your subscription and open and download the initial page of the channel.

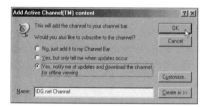

No sooner does Windows close the Add Active Channel (TM) content dialog box than it takes you to the opening page of the channel. You can then explore all of its content areas at your leisure.

After you finish surfing your new channel, you can return to the Microsoft Channel Guide by positioning the mouse on the left side of the browsing area to get the sliding Channel bar to make an appearance. Alternatively, if you want to fix it on the screen, click the Fullscreen button on the Standard Buttons bar (the one to the immediate right of the Channels button with the radar dish) to fix the Channel Explorer bar in its own frame.

Customizing the channel subscription settings

You may not always want to use the default subscription settings when adding a new channel. For example, you may want to limit the amount of new content that's automatically downloaded to your computer, want an e-mail message sent to you every time the channel is updated, or want to change the schedule for downloading new contents.

To customize the subscription settings when subscribing to a new channel, follow these steps:

1. In the Add Active Channel(TM) content dialog box that appears after clicking the Add Active Channel button on the channel preview, click the Customize button to open the first dialog box of the Channel Subscription wizard.

In the first dialog box of the Channel Subscription wizard, you can choose between downloading just the home (first) page of the channel and the (default) option of downloading all the pages specified by the channel developer (which can become quite a download in the channels that have loads of content).

2. If you want to limit the channel downloads to the initial page, choose the Download only the channel home page radio button before clicking the Next button.

The next dialog box of the Channel Subscription wizard gives you an opportunity to be sent an e-mail message notifying you that the channel's contents have changed. This e-mail message contains a hyperlink that, when clicked, opens the channel, enabling you to view its contents offline.

3. Choose the Yes, send an e-mail message to the following address radio button to be informed of updates to the channel by e-mail. In addition, the regular "gleam" that's added to the channel's icon informs you of updates. (When you choose this radio button, the Change Address button becomes active, which you can then use to edit or add your e-mail address, if necessary.) Otherwise, leave the No button selected when you click the Next button.

The next dialog box of the Channel Subscription wizard gives you an opportunity to override the update schedule assigned by the channel developer. You can choose between a completely manual update system wherein channel content is updated *only* when you specifically request it and a regularly scheduled update system of your own choosing.

4. Choose the Manually radio button to have channel content downloaded only when you choose the Update Now or Update All command. If you want to have content downloaded on a set schedule other than the one designated by the channel developer, leave the Scheduled radio button selected and then select a new update interval (Daily, Monthly, or Weekly) in the drop-down list box immediately below this radio button.

5. Click the Finish button to close the Channel Subscription Wizard dialog box and return to the Subscribe dialog box.

6. Click OK in the Add Active Channel(TM) content dialog box.

When you click the OK button after customizing your settings with the Channel Subscription wizard, Windows connects you to the home page of the channel, where you can start exploring its contents.

If after using the customized subscription settings, you decide that they still need some tweaking, you can change any of these custom settings by choosing the Properties command from the channel's shortcut menu. To open the shortcut menu for a channel, right-click its icon in the Channel or Favorites Explorer bar in the browsing window.

See "Subscribing to Web Pages" earlier in this part.

Subscribing to Web Sites

See "Adding to your Favorites."

Viewing Active Channels

To view the updated contents for the channels to which you've subscribed, you open the Active Channel Viewer (or just Channel Viewer, for short). The Channel Viewer is simply a special view of the Internet Explorer with a sliding Channel Explorer bar (also known as the Channel bar, for short) and the full-screen viewing mode turned so that the Standard Buttons bar is the only toolbar displayed, and its buttons are shown without any captions.

The sliding Channel bar in the Channel Viewer automatically appears whenever you position the mouse pointer somewhere over the area of the underlying Web page that the bar occupies when displayed. And just as automatically, it disappears whenever you position the mouse pointer somewhere on the underlying Web page to the right of the Channel bar.

If you want, you can keep the Channel bar displayed at all times in the Channel Viewer by clicking the thumbtack icon in the upper-right corner of its title bar (so that it appears "pressed"). When you click the thumbtack icon, Channel Viewer fixes the Channel bar in a frame on the left side, while simultaneously displaying the contents of the current Web page in its own frame (in most cases, complete with scroll bars) on the right.

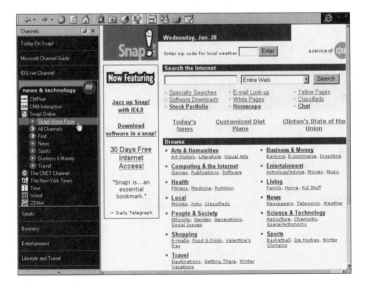

To close the fixed Channel bar so that the Web page in the frame on the right is then displayed in a single, full-screen frame, click the Channels button on the Standard Buttons bar or the Close button in the upper-left corner of the Channel title bar. To redisplay the fixed Channel bar so that you can select different channel pages, click the Channels button again.

If you want to be able to view the current Web page at full-screen screen size and return the Channel bar to its original sliding modus operandi, click the thumbtack icon in its title bar (so that it no longer appears pressed).

Opening the Channel Viewer

In opening the Channel Viewer, you have a choice among several methods:

✦ Click the View Channels button in the Quick Launch toolbar on the Windows taskbar. This action opens the Welcome to the Active Channel Viewer page.

✦ Click a particular channel button in the Internet Explorer Channel bar on the Windows desktop, assuming that the View as Web Page setting is turned on (by right-clicking the desktop and then choosing Active Desktop➪View as Web Page). This action displays the initial Web page of the channel you select in the Channel Viewer.

✦ In one of the three browsing windows, choose View➪ Explorer Bar➪Channels, or click the Channels button on the Standard Buttons bar if you are browsing Web pages. This action splits the browsing window by fixing the Channel bar in a frame on the left side and the contents of the Web page or folder you're currently browsing in a frame on the right. To remove the frames and revert to the sliding Channel bar, click the Channel Guide or one of the other channel buttons in the fixed Channel Explorer bar and then click the Fullscreen button on the Standard Buttons bar.

Selecting the channel pages to view

After you open the Channel Viewer, you can view the pages of a particular channel (to which you are already subscribed) by clicking its button on the Channel bar. As soon as you click the button, the Channel bar opens to display the hyperlinks to individual pages of the channel, and the home page of the channel is displayed in the browsing window.

To display a particular page within the channel, simply click its hyperlink in the Channel bar or use the controls provided on the home page. (Many channels provide a variety of page controls courtesy of dynamic HTML.) When you have the channel page you want displayed in the browsing window, you can remove the Channel bar (either by moving the mouse off of the bar or, if the bar is fixed, by clicking the Channels Button on the Standard Buttons toolbar).

You can view channels from one of the three browsing windows by selecting them from the Favorites pull-down menu or on the Favorites Explorer bar (which you display by choosing View⇨Explorer Bar⇨Favorites).

To select a channel from the Favorites pull-down menu, highlight the Channels folder icon and then click the name of the channel you want to view in the submenu that appears.

To select a channel on the Favorites Explorer bar, click the Channels folder icon on the Explorer bar and then click the name of the channel you want to view in the expanded list.

Viewing TV Channels

If your computer is equipped with a TV tuner card and you have connected it to some sort of TV antenna, cable box, or satellite dish, you can watch television programs in a window on your computer's desktop. Windows 98 includes an online TV Viewer, called Microsoft WebTV for Windows, that makes it easy to find out what's on TV and select the program that you want to watch.

If you add a TV tuner card to your computer after Windows 98 has been installed, you will probably have to add the WebTV for Windows software to your current Windows installation. To add this software, put the Windows 98 CD-ROM in your CD-ROM drive and then click the Add/Remove button in the lower-right corner of the Windows 98 CD-ROM window. Select the WebTV for Windows check box near the bottom of the Components list box on the Windows Setup tab in the Add/Remove Programs Properties dialog box before clicking OK.

You can always tell when the TV Viewer software is installed, because Windows adds a Launch TV Viewer button to the Quick Launch toolbar on the Taskbar. You click this button when you want to open the TV Viewer, either to consult the programming guide or to watch a TV program. Note that when you install the WebTV for Windows software, in addition to the Launch TV Viewer button on the Quick Launch toolbar, Windows adds a Broadcast button to the Internet Explorer Channel Bar on the Active Desktop.

You can use the Broadcast button to subscribe to channels like TV Quest and Microsoft Broadcast Network which download daily the TV program schedules for the local TV stations and cable provider(s) in your area.

Downloading the local programming to the Program Guide

The first thing you will want to do with Microsoft WebTV for Windows is download a listing of the channels and TV programming for your local area. Windows enables you to do this by providing a hyperlink to Microsoft's StarSight Web site, from which you can download the local broadcast or cable programming.

To download the local programming information from this Web site (assuming that you have Internet access and some way to get connected), follow these steps:

1. Click the Launch TV Viewer button on the Quick Launch toolbar.

The first time you click this button, Windows opens the Welcome to WebTV for Windows screen and starts playing an audio track explaining what you can do with the Program Guide.

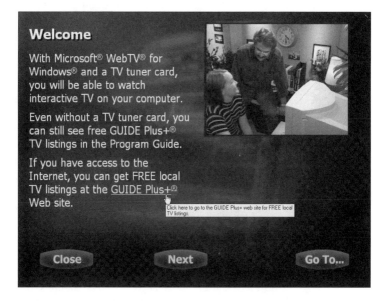

2. On the Welcome screen, click the Guide Plus+ hyperlink to connect to the Internet and open the Welcome to Setup browsing window on the Microsoft Web site.

3. Type your zip code in the Postal Code text box (click the Yes button if you get an alert box warning you that you are about to send information over the Internet).

Windows then opens a Choose Broadcast or Cable system page that displays your broadcast area or cable providers.

4. Click the name of your cable provider or, if you don't have cable TV, click the hyperlink for your broadcast area.

5. Click Yes in the alert box warning you about the ActiveX object on the page in order to close the alert box. Then click the Download button in the TV Program Listing Data Downloader box.

Windows then downloads the programming information for your cable provider or broadcast area.

6. When the Status in the TV Program Listing Data Downloader box reads Success! Loader has completed, click the Close box in the upper-right corner of the Welcome window to close this window and return to the Welcome page of the TV Viewer.

7. Click the Close button on the lower-left to close the Welcome screen and replace it with the Program Guide part of the TV Viewer, complete with the channels and program listing you just downloaded.

The listings that you download from the StarSight Web site are only current for the day on which you do the download. To obtain the current listings for another day, you must repeat the preceding steps. To display the page with the StarSight hyperlink after launching Windows 98 TV Viewer, click the TVC button in the Program Guide to select the TV Configuration channel; then click the WATCH button in the onscreen TV remote.

Selecting the TV channel you want to watch

After you download the program listings from the StarSight Web site, you can consult the Microsoft WebTV for Windows' Program Guide to select the program you want to watch. The Guide tab in the TV Viewer enables you to scroll through the program listings by time and by channel.

✦ To scroll up and down through the channels, drag the scroll button up or down or click the up or down scroll arrows in the Program Guide's vertical scroll bar. You can also scroll up and down one channel at a time by pressing the ↑ and ↓ keys, or up one page and down one page by pressing the PgUp and PgDn keys.

✦ To scroll left and right through the time of day, drag the scroll button left or right or click the left or right scroll arrows in the Program Guide's horizontal scroll bar. You can also scroll forward and backward a program at a time by pressing the → and ← keys.

✦ To display programs for a certain period of the day, click the pop-up button on the right of the button that contains a description of the current period of the day (Morning, Afternoon, Evening, and so on) and then select the period you want displayed on the pop-up menu. To display the programs that are on currently, click Now on the pop-up menu.

✦ To restrict the listing of the programs to only those channels that you designated as your favorites, click the pop-up button on the right of the All Channels button and then click Favorites on the pop-up menu.

GUIDE	SEARCH		
Sat Feb 28 ▼	Afternoon ▼	All Channels ▼	Microsoft
1 PM	1:30	2 PM	2:30

		1 PM	1:30	2 PM	2:30
2	HBO	Aspen Extreme		Sabrina	
3	ESPN	NASCAR Busch Grand National Series			
4	KRON	Notre Dame at Providence		Jeep King of the Mo Downhill	
5	max	Some Kind of Wonderful			Head
6	KFTY	Paid Programmi...	Paid Programmi...	Paid Programmi...	Paid Progr
7	KGO	National Geographi...	TV.COM	USC at Washington	
8	KTVU	Chicago Blackhawks at Colorado Avalanche			
9	KQED	Cooking With Cura	Mollie Katzenla C	Home Cooking W	Great Cura

webtv. for Windows

National Geographic: On Assignment
Educational
12:30 PM - 1:30 PM
NR(Not Rated)

Loggerhead turtles; Cayman Islands diving.

OTHER TIMES

Why click here? **TRIBUNE** desktop

Sat Feb 28
1:21 pm

When you find a program that you might be interested in watching, click its name in the Program Guide to display a short description of the program's content, its running time, and its rating. This information appears on the on-screen TV Viewer remote that appears to the immediate right of the Program Guide.

 Many TV programs have Web sites that follow their plot lines, features, or characters, or some combination. To display a page of hyperlinks to Web sites related to a particular program in the Program Guide, click the hyperlink attached to the program's name near the top of the TV Viewer on-screen remote.

Also, keep in mind that you can get online help with using Microsoft WebTV for Windows at any time by pressing F10 to display the TV toolbar and then clicking the Help button.

Watching a TV program

When you find a program that you want to watch, you can start watching by taking these two steps:

1. In the Program Guide, find the number of the channel showing the program you want to watch.

2. Press F10 to display the TV toolbar; then enter the number of the channel on the program guide text box. Then press enter.

After you finish watching TV and using the Program Guide, close the TV Viewer by pressing F10 or by positioning the mouse at the top of the screen until the TV toolbar appears and then clicking its Close button in the upper-right corner.

Searching for programs

You can use the Search tab in the Program Guide to find programs that you might want to watch. To search for programs in a particular area, follow these steps:

1. Click the Launch TV Viewer button on the Quick Launch toolbar to open the Program Guide.

2. Click the Search tab in the Program Guide.

3. Click the name of the category you want to watch (such as Action, Comedy, Drama, and so on) in the Categories area on the left.

As soon as you choose a category, the TV Viewer lists all the programs on that day that fall into that category. To get a description of a particular program and information on when the program is on, click the program of interest in this list. The TV Viewer then displays this information in the on-screen TV Viewer remote to the right.

4. To view the program (if it's on at the time you perform the search), press F10 and then enter the channel number in the Program Guide text box. Then press Enter. To set a reminder to watch the program (if it's on sometime later in the day), click the Remind button on the TV Viewer remote instead; then select the Once radio button and enter in the text box of the Remind dialog box the number of minutes in advance that you want to be reminded.

When you set a reminder for viewing a program, the reminder appears on-screen in a dialog box however many minutes before the program starts that you designated in the Reminder dialog box.

To check the reminders that you set up, click My Reminders at the bottom of the Categories list on the Search tab of the Program Guide.

To cancel a program reminder, select the program on the Search tab and then click the Remind button on the on-screen TV Viewer remote. Next, select the No Reminder radio button.

Adding your favorite channels

If you have favorite TV channels that you watch regularly, you can add buttons to the TV toolbar for selecting them (as long you don't have more than five favorite channels).

To add a favorite TV channel to the TV toolbar, take these steps:

1. Launch the TV Viewer; then use the Program Guide to find out the number of the channel you wish to add. (*See* "Selecting the TV channel you want to watch" and "Watching a TV program" earlier in this part for details.)

2. If the TV toolbar is not visible, press F10 or position the mouse at the top of the screen until the toolbar appears.

If you have a cable box or set top box attached to your computer's TV tuner, you can also display the TV toolbar by pressing the Guide button or Menu button on your TV remote. Be sure, however, that you point the TV remote at the box and not at the computer screen when you press this button.

3. Enter the number of the channel to add in the Program Guide text box; then press enter and click the Add button on the TV toolbar.

After you add a channel to the TV toolbar, you can switch to that channel and watch whatever program is on simply by clicking its button. (Remember that you can always display the TV toolbar by pressing F10 from anywhere within the TV Viewer program.)

To remove a channel from the TV toolbar, select the channel (preferably by clicking its button on the toolbar) and then click the Remove button on the TV toolbar. (The Remove button automatically replaces the Add button for channels that are already on the TV toolbar.)

Windows Update

The Windows Update command on the Start menu provides an almost completely automated method for keeping your Windows 98 operating system software up-to-date. As soon as you choose the Windows Update command on the Start menu, Windows puts you online and connects you to the Windows Update Web page on the Microsoft Web site.

To have your computer checked out to see if you are in need of some updated Windows components, follow these steps:

1. On the Windows Update Web page, click the Update Wizard hyperlink and click the Yes button if a Security Alert dialog box appears.

2. After the information in the Web page redraws, click the Update Wizard hyperlink to have your computer checked for out-of-date software components.

When you click the Update hyperlink, the Welcome To Microsoft Windows Update Wizard Web page opens, and the Update Wizard checks your computer for needed updates. After checking your system, a list of possible updates appears in the Available Updates list box.

3. To have the Update Wizard install a particular update, click its name in the Available Updates list box to display a description of the update in the Description list box, then click the Install hyperlink that appears above both of these list boxes.

After you click the Install button, the Update Wizard down-loads and installs the updated files for the component you selected.

4. Repeat Step 3 until you have installed all of the available updates that you want added to your system.

5. Click the Close box in the upper-right corner of the Welcome To Microsoft Windows Update Wizard Web page and the Windows Update Web page to close both Web pages in their browser windows.

TIP

You can remove an update and restore your computer to its previous state by choosing Update Windows on the Windows Start menu and then clicking the Restore hyperlink in the Windows Update Web page on the Microsoft Web site.

Doing Everyday Stuff in Windows 98

Part III contains a pretty complete laundry list of all the essential "things to do" in Windows 98. You find out about such elementary stuff as how to control the icons on your desktop, add and remove software and printers, regulate and dispense with the files and folders that manage to clutter your hard drive, launch your programs, obtain online help, and even safely shut down the whole Windows kit and caboodle.

In this part . . .

- ✔ Making copies of your really important files

- ✔ Creating new folders to hold the copies of your really important files

- ✔ Finding the folders that hold the copies of your really important files

- ✔ Opening the copies of really important files after you've located their folders

- ✔ Starting all the hundreds of programs that you run under Windows 98

- ✔ Printing files from Windows 98, installing new printers, and managing your print jobs

- ✔ Shutting down and getting the heck out of Windows 98 after a long day of using all the hundreds of programs you run under Windows 98

. . . and much, much more!

Arranging and Sizing Icons in a Window

When browsing local files in any of three browsing windows (My Computer, Windows Explorer, and Internet Explorer 4), you can modify the size of the icons used to represent files and folders as well as determine how much (if any) information about them is displayed.

To change the way icons appear in any of these windows, choose from the following commands on the window's View pull-down menu. Note that the same menu options appear when you right-click in the window to display its shortcut menu:

✦ **Large Icons (the default):** Displays the largest version of the folder and file icons, with their names below.

✦ **Small Icons:** Displays a smaller version of the folder and file icons, with their names on the right side of the icons.

✦ **List:** Uses the same icons as the Small Icons option except that the icons with their folders and filenames are arranged in a single column along the left side of the window.

✦ **Details:** Adds columns of additional information (like a description, or the file type, file size, and so on) to the arrangement used when you select the List option.

Switch to the Small Icons viewing option when you need to see as much of the window's contents as possible. Switch to the Details viewing option when you need to get as much information as possible about the files and folders in a window.

After you decide how file and folder icons appear in a window, you can also choose how they are arranged. Choose View➪Arrange Icons and select from the following options on the Arrange Icons submenu:

✦ **by Name:** Sort icons alphabetically by name.

✦ **by Type:** Sort icons by file type.

✦ **by Size:** Sort icons by size, from smallest to largest.

✦ **by Date:** Sort icons by date, from oldest to most recent.

✦ **Auto Arrange:** Let Windows sort icons by the default setting (which happens to be by type).

When you select the My Computer level (the second from the very top level of any local system) on the Address bar's drop-down list in one of the three browsing windows, Windows replaces the Name and Date options on the Arrange Icons menu with these commands:

✦ **by Drive Letter:** Gives precedence to icons that represent hard drives, floppy drives, CD-ROM drives, and so on that may be part of your system or available on a Local Area Network (LAN).

✦ **by Free Space:** Sort drive icons by available free space.

When you point to a menu command, the status bar at the bottom of the window displays a description of what that command does.

These methods of arranging icons in windows are pretty old hat to most Windows users. To give your window icons a complete make-over courtesy of Web integration in Windows 98, *see* "Changing the Folder Options for Windows 98" in Part II and "Icons" in Part I.

Copying (and Moving) Files and Folders

Copying and moving files and folders in Windows 98 is accomplished by using the two universal methods described in this section — drag-and-drop and copy/cut-and-paste.

Drag 'em up, drop 'em down

The art of drag-and-drop is simplicity itself and requires only that you do the following:

1. Select the object you want to copy or move. *See* "These icons are made for clicking . . ." in Part I and "Selecting Files and Folders" later in this part for more on the new techniques Windows 98 provides for selecting objects with the mouse.

2. While continuing to hold down the mouse button, drag the object to a new location.

3. When you arrive at the desired location, release the mouse button to drop the object there.

To copy files with drag-and-drop, follow these steps:

1. Open the window that contains the items to be copied, as well as the window with the folder or disk to which you want to copy the items.

2. Select all the items to be copied. You can do this by drawing a bounding box around the file icons when they all fit into a rectangular shape.

3. Hold down the Ctrl key as you drag the selected items to the folder to which you want to copy them.

4. When the destination folder icon is selected (that is, high-lighted), drop the selected items by releasing the mouse button.

The flavors of copy-and-paste

The copy and paste commands, like many of the everyday tasks in Windows 98, can be performed by either selecting commands on the menu bar or by using keyboard combination shortcuts. To copy files with copy-and-paste, using either method, follow these steps:

1. Open a browsing window that holds the items to be copied.

2. Select all the items to be copied and then choose Edit➪Copy, or press Ctrl+C.

3. Open a browsing window that holds the folder or disk where the copied items are to appear.

4. Open the folder or disk to hold the copied items and then choose Edit➪Paste, or press Ctrl+V.

Use drag-and-drop to copy when you have both the folder with the items to be copied and the destination folder or disk displayed on the desktop (as when using the Windows Explorer). Use copy-and-paste to copy when you can't easily display both the folder with the items to be copied and the destination folder or disk together on the desktop (as with My Computer or Internet Explorer 4).

If all you want to do is back up some files from your hard drive to a floppy disk in drive A or B, you can do so with the Send To command. After selecting the files to copy, just open the shortcut menu attached to one of the file icons and then choose the correct floppy drive, such as 5^1/$_4$ Floppy (A) or (B), or 3 ^{1}/$_2$ Floppy (A) or (B) on the Send To menu. Oh, and one thing more: Don't forget to insert a diskette, preferably already formatted and ready to go, before you start this little operation.

Move over folders and files

You can move files and folders in the Windows Explorer by using either the drag-and-drop or the cut-and-paste method. To move an object using drag-and-drop, follow these steps:

1. Open a browsing window that contains the folders and files that you want to move. If you're just moving some files in a folder, be sure to open that folder in the window.

2. Open a browsing window that displays the icon for the folder or disk to which the files and folders you're about to select in the first folder (described in Step 1) will be moved.

3. Select in the first window all the files and folders that you want to move.

4. Drag the selected files and folders from the first window to the window that contains the destination folder or disk (the one where the files are to be moved).

5. As soon as you select the icon of the destination folder or disk (indicated by a highlighted name), release the mouse button to move the files into that folder or disk.

When you drag files or folders from one disk to another, Windows 98 automatically copies the files and folders rather than moving them (meaning that you must still delete them from their original disk if you need the space).

Drag-and-drop moving from folder to folder is great because it's really fast. This method does have a major drawback, however: It's pretty easy to drop your file icons into the wrong folder. Instead of having a cow when you open up what you thought was the destination folder and find that your files are gone, you can locate them by using the Find Files or Folders command (**see** "Finding Files and Folders").

Moving files and folders via cut-and-paste ensures that the lost files scenario just described won't happen, though it's much clunkier than the elegant drag-and-drop method. To move files and folders with cut-and-paste, use these steps:

1. Open a window that displays all the files and folders you want to move.

2. Select all the files and folders you want to move.

3. Choose Edit⇨Cut, or press Ctrl+X, to cut the selected files and place them on the Clipboard.

4. Open a window that contains the destination folder or disk (the one to which you want to move the selected files or folders).

5. Choose Edit⇨Paste in the window where the selected stuff is to be moved, or press Ctrl+V, to insert the files into the folder or disk.

Use the drag-and-drop method when on the desktop you can see both the files and folders to be moved and the folder to which you are moving them. Switch to the cut-and-paste method when you cannot see both.

Remember: Windows automatically moves files when you drag their file icons from one folder to another on the same disk and copies files (indicated by the appearance of a plus sign next to the pointer) when you drag their icons from one disk to another.

When using the cut and paste commands to move files or folders, you don't have to keep open the first window in which they were originally located after you cut them. Just be sure that you paste cut files or folders in a location before you choose Edit⇨Copy or Edit⇨Cut again in Windows 98.

See also "Windows Explorer" in Part I for more on copying and "Selecting Files and Folders" later in this part for information about selecting files and folders in a window.

Creating New Files and Folders

Create empty folders to hold your files and empty files to hold new documents of a particular type, right within Windows 98.

To create an empty folder, follow these steps:

1. Open the folder inside a browsing window in which the new folder is to appear.

2. Choose File⇨New⇨Folder from the menu bar or New⇨Folder on the window's shortcut menu.

3. Replace the temporary folder name (New Folder) by typing a name of your choosing and pressing Enter.

To create an empty file of a certain type, follow these steps:

1. Open the window and the folder where the new file is required.

2. Choose File⇨New from the menu bar or New on the window's shortcut menu.

3. Choose the type of file you want to create (such as Microsoft PowerPoint Presentation, Microsoft Excel Worksheet, Microsoft Word Document, Microsoft Access Database, Wave Sound, Text Document, or Briefcase, and so on) from the New submenu.

4. Replace the temporary filename (such as New Microsoft Word Document) by typing a name of your choosing and pressing Enter.

You can use your freshly created icon to open its associated program. *See* "Launching Programs" later in this part.

Create a new folder when you need to have a new place to store your files and other folders. Create an empty file when you want to create an empty file in a particular folder before you put something in it.

See also "Let's hear it for long filenames" in Part I and "Renaming Files" later in this part for information on naming new files and folders in Window 98.

Creating Shortcuts

See "Shortcuts" in Part I.

Deleting Junk

Because the whole purpose of working on computers is to create junk, you need to know how to get rid of unneeded files and folders to free up space on your hard drive. To delete files or folders, follow these steps:

1. In one of the three browsing windows, open the folder that holds the files or folders to be deleted.

2. Select all the files and folders to be deleted.

3. Choose File⇨Delete on the menu bar or press the Delete key. (You can also drag the selected items to the Recycle Bin.)

4. Choose the Yes button in the Confirm File Delete dialog box that asks if you want to send the selected file or files to the Recycle Bin.

Windows 98 puts all items that you delete in the Recycle Bin. To get rid of all the items in the Recycle Bin, do the following:

1. Open the Desktop level (the very top level on any computer system) on the Address bar's drop-down list in one of the three browsing windows or select the Recycle Bin icon on the Windows desktop. Then choose Empty Recycle Bin from the Recycle Bin's shortcut menu. You can also empty the Recycle Bin by opening its icon and then clicking the Empty Recycle Bin hyperlink in the Recycle Bin window's info panel (if you don't see the info panel with this hyperlink, choose View⇨ As Web Page from the window's menu bar).

2. Click the Yes button or press Enter in the Confirm File Delete or Confirm Multiple File Delete dialog box that asks if you want to delete the selected file or files. Be aware, however, that there's no turning back from this step.

Get rid of stuff in the Recycle Bin only when you're absolutely sure that you're never going to need it again (or you have backed up the files on diskettes or some other media, such as tapes or CD-ROMs).

If you hold down the Shift key when you press the Delete key, Windows displays the Confirm File Delete dialog box that asks if you want to delete the selected file or files, rather than the dialog box asking if you want to send the files to the Recycle Bin.

You can restore all the items that you have exiled to the Recycle Bin any time prior to emptying the Bin by opening the Recycle Bin in any of the three browsing windows or from the Windows desktop. Then you click the <u>Restore All</u> hyperlink in the Recycle Bin window's info panel (if you don't see this hyperlink, choose View⇨As Web Page on the window's menu bar).

See also "Recycle Bin" in Part I and "Uninstalling Programs," later in this part, for information on getting rid of a program.

Doing DOS Stuff

For those Windows users who find themselves longing for the good old days when you used DOS to get things done on a computer, Windows 98 enables you to open a window with the DOS prompt so that you can type away your nostalgia.

Everything you need to know about using DOS:

+ To open a window to DOS within Windows 98 in an MS-DOS Prompt window, click the Start button on the taskbar and then choose <u>P</u>rograms⇨MS-DOS Prompt.

+ To restart your computer in DOS mode (heaven forbid!) rather than in Windows 98, click the Start button on the taskbar and then choose Sh<u>u</u>t Down on the Start menu to open the Shut Down Windows dialog box. Select the Restart in <u>M</u>S-DOS Mode radio button in the Shut Down Windows dialog box and then click the OK button.

+ To return to Windows 98 after restarting in MS-DOS mode, type **exit** at the DOS prompt and then press Enter. To close the MS-DOS Prompt window, you can either type **exit** and press Enter or you can click the window's Close box.

 Don't fool around with DOS commands unless you are really sure of what you're doing. If you ever get a DOS window open and then get cold feet, just click the Close button in the MS-DOS Prompt window to close it and get back to Windows 98 where you belong.

Finding Files, Folders, and Other Stuff

The Find feature enables you to quickly locate all those misplaced files and folders that you're just sure are hiding somewhere on your hard drive.

To open the Find window to search for a file or folder, follow these steps:

1. Click the Start button on the taskbar and then choose <u>F</u>ind⇨<u>F</u>iles or Folders on the Start menu. This action opens the Find: All Files window.

2. Enter the search conditions and where to look in the appropriate tabs of the Find: All Files window (Name & Location, Date, and Advanced).

3. Click the F<u>i</u>nd Now button to start the search.

When Windows 98 completes a search, it expands the Find dialog box to display in a list box all the files that meet your search conditions (as shown in the preceding figure). This list box shows the name, location, size, type, and the date the file was last modified. If this information isn't enough for you to make a positive ID on the file, use the Quick View command on the file icon's shortcut menu to take a gander at the file's contents (*see* "Getting a Preview of a File's Contents" later in this part).

Letting 'em know what you're searching for

The Find dialog box contains three tabs (Name & Location, Date, and Advanced), with various options with which you set the search conditions to use for your search. On the tabs in the Find dialog box, you find these options:

Name & Location Tab Options	What They Do
Named	Enter all or part of the file or folder name you're looking for in this edit box. Don't worry about capitalization. Windows remembers the stuff you enter in this edit box so that you can reselect search text in the drop-down list box.
Containing text	Use this edit box to specify a string of characters, a word, or a phrase that should be contained within the files you're looking for.
Look in	Use this drop-down list box or the Browse button to select the drive where you want to conduct the search.
Include subfolders	Normally, Windows searches all the folders within the folders on the disk specified in the Look In edit box. If you're pretty sure that the files and folders you want won't be found any deeper than in the first level of folders, remove the check mark from this check box.

Date Tab Options	What They Do
All files	Normally, Windows automatically selects this radio button and searches all files in the location specified in the Look In text box on the Name & Location tab.
Find all files	Select this radio button and its Created, Modified, or Last accessed options from the drop-down list to find files or folders created, modified, or accessed between certain dates or within the last few days or months (see the following options).
between and	Select this radio button and enter the two dates between which the files or folders must have been created, edited, or accessed. The two dates you enter in the between text boxes are included in the search.
during the previous month(s)	Select this radio button and enter the number of months in the text box during which files and folders were created, modified, or accessed.
during the previous days	Select this radio button and enter the number of days in the text box during which files and folders were created, modified, or accessed.

Advanced Tab Options	What They Do
Of type	Use this drop-down list box to specify a particular type of file to search for (rather than All Files and Folders, which is the default).
Size is	Select the At least or At most option in the drop-down list box and enter the number of kilobytes (KB) that the size of the files to be searched must have attained or not exceeded.

Keep in mind that the search conditions you cook up with the Name & Location, Date, and Advanced tabs of the Find dialog box are cumulative. For example, if you want to find all files and folders created within the last six days but the name **klondike** is still entered in the Named text box of the Name & Location tab, Windows searches only for files and folders that use the name klondike in their file and folder names and that have been created or modified within the last six days. To find all the files, regardless of what they're called, you need to delete **klondike** from the Named text box and then choose the Find Now button again.

If you want to return all the search settings to their default values before you conduct another search, choose the New Search button in the Find dialog box and then choose OK in the Find Files alert box.

The Find feature in Windows 98 is so quick (even when searching an entire hard drive that's just chock-full of junk) that I urge you to use it whenever you have the least little bit of trouble locating a file or folder (rather than waste a bunch of time wading through even the more likely files and folders). Keep in mind that you don't have to know the name of the file to use the Find feature, because Windows 98 can search for specific text in a file if you use the Containing text box on the Name & Location tab of the Find dialog box.

Finding lost computers, Web sites, and people

Files and folders aren't the only things that you can search for with the Find command. In addition, you can use the Computer option to search for computers to which you have access when your computer is connected to a LAN, you can also use the On the Internet option to find Web sites (*see* "Doing an all-in-one search" in Part II for details). Finally, you can use the People option to locate people that you've either entered in your own address book or who are listed in one of the online directories included in Windows 98.

To find a computer on your Local Area Network, choose Find⇨Computer from the Start menu to open the Find: Computer dialog box. Then enter the name of the computer in the Named text box before you click the Find Now button.

To use the Find⇨People command to search for someone listed in your address book or in a number of different online directories, follow these steps:

1. Click the Start button on the taskbar and then choose Find⇨People to open the Find People dialog box.

2. Click the name of the source or directory you want to search in the Look-In drop-down list (Address Book, Yahoo! People Search, Bigfoot, InfoSpace, InfoSpace Business, Switchboard, VeriSign, or WhoWhere).

3. Enter either the name or the e-mail address of the person you want to find in the appropriate text box.

   Note that when you search the address book, you can also search for the person by his or her mailing address, telephone number, or some comment that you've entered about the person.

4. Click the Find Now button to begin searching your Address Book or the online directory you selected.

   Note that when you search one of the online directories, such as InfoSpace, Windows connects you to its directory on the Internet before beginning the search. After Windows finishes searching the Address Book or online directory, the results of the search appear at the bottom of an expanded Find People dialog box.

5. If you find the person you were searching for in one of the online directories and want to add him or her to your address book, click the person's listing to select it and then click the Add to Address Book button.

6. When you finish your people searching, click the Close button in the upper-right corner of the Find People dialog box.

Formatting a Disk

If you bought a box of disks at an incredibly good price, chances are that they are unformatted. You must format diskettes before you can save files and folders on them.

To format a diskette in drive A of your computer, follow these steps:

1. Insert a blank diskette or a diskette that holds files and folders that you don't give a hoot about.

2. Open the My Computer window and then right-click the icon for the Floppy Drive (A:).

3. Select the Format command from the A: drive's shortcut menu to open the Format dialog box.

4. By default, Windows 98 selects high density [1.44MB (3.5")] as the Capacity for the size of the diskette you're formatting. Choose the lesser (double-density) capacity [720K (3.5")] if you inserted that kind of diskette into your floppy drive.

5. By default, Windows 98 chooses Quick (erase) as the Format Type. Quick (erase) is the option of choice when you're reformatting a disk that contains files and folders that you no longer need. If you're formatting a brand new diskette, choose the Full radio button. Choose the Copy system files only radio button if you want to copy system files to a disk that is already formatted.

6. (Optional) Enter a label in the Label text box, or, if you decide not to use the label entered in the Label text box, you can select the No Label check box.

7. (Optional) Remove the check mark from the Display summary when finished check box if you don't want to see a Format Results dialog box that gives you the lowdown on the disk's storage status after the formatting is completed. (This status includes information such as total capacity, bytes in bad sectors, and bytes used by the system.)

8. (Optional) Choose Copy System Files if you want to copy system files to the disk after it's been formatted.

9. Click the Start button to begin formatting the disk.

After you click Start, Windows keeps you informed of its progress in the Formatting box at the bottom of the Format dialog box. If you need to stop the process before it's complete, click the Cancel button.

When the diskette formatting is finished, click the Close button or press Enter to close the Format dialog box. If you want to format another diskette of the same type, replace the newly formatted diskette with another that needs formatting and click the Start button (or press Enter) to begin formatting it.

Be sure to match the capacity setting to the physical type of disk you're using: double-density [720K (3.5")] or high-density [1.44 MB (3.5")].

You can also format a brand-new, never-been-formatted, right-out-of-the-box diskette by inserting it in its disk drive and then opening the drive icon in the My Computer window. Windows 98 displays an alert box containing this message:

```
The disk in drive A is not formatted. Do you want
    to format it now?
```

Click the Yes button or press Enter to open the Format dialog box, where you can specify the disk capacity, format type, label, and so on before you start the formatting by clicking the Start button.

Getting a Preview of a File's Contents

Quick View enables you to have a fast look-see into the contents of certain types of files before you open them. To preview a file's contents, right-click the file's icon and select Quick View from its shortcut menu. Note that if the file's shortcut menu doesn't have a Quick View command, that file is of a type that you can't preview with the Quick View feature.

If the file contains a graphic or is an HTML document, however, you can preview its contents with the Thumbnail view (*see* "Browsing folders with Thumbnail view turned on" in Part II for details on how to select this view). Also, you can display a thumbnail of a graphic or HTML file in the info panel, if you select the file icon when Web Page view is turned on in the browsing window (*see* "Browsing folders with Web Page view turned on" in Part II for details on how to use this view).

To open a file from the Quick View window so that you can edit it, click the Open File for Editing button on the window's toolbar or choose File⇔Open File for Editing. To use Quick View to snoop in a bunch of different files without opening separate windows for each file, click the Replace Window button on the window's toolbar or choose View⇔Replace Window.

Getting Help

Microsoft has vastly improved its online help with the introduction of Windows Help in Windows 98. Windows Help is now an HTML document with links and buttons that you can use to:

✦ Search for help topics by category and name.

✦ Find out all about Windows 98 with the online version of the Microsoft Windows 98 Getting Started book.

◆ Connect to the Web and get specific information and software updates.

◆ Troubleshoot your system.

To open Windows Help, follow these steps:

1. Click the Start button on the taskbar and then choose Help on the Start menu to open the Windows Help window.

2. To select a help topic in the list box of the Contents tab, click the topic (preceded by a closed book icon) to expand all of its subtopics (preceded by a document with a question mark). Then click the subtopic to display its steps in the frame on the right, as you see in the following figure.

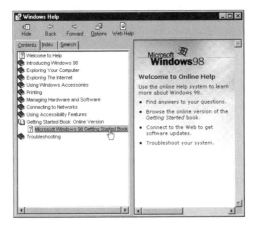

3. To select a help topic on the Index tab, click this tab and then select any entry in the text box at the top and replace it with the first few characters of the subject you want help on. When Windows selects the topic you're interested in, click the Display button at the bottom to display its information in the frame on the right.

4. To select a help topic on the Search tab, type the name of the topic you need help on in the text box at the top and then click the List Topics button to display related topics in the Topic list box below. Select the topic you want information on in the Topic list box and then click the <u>D</u>isplay button at the bottom to display its information in the frame on the right.

5. To print the Help topic displayed in the frame on the right, click the <u>O</u>ptions button and then select <u>P</u>rint from the pop-up menu. If you choose the Print command with the Contents tab selected, you get the option to print the current page, or all topics under the selected book, or the entire Help contents. To quickly print the current help topic, right-click the display frame and choose Print from the shortcut menu.

6. Click the window's Close button to close the Windows Help window.

You can narrow much of the online help in Windows 98 to the task at hand by selecting the Help or ? button that appears in the dialog box or window you have open. Leave the searching for topics in the Windows Help dialog box to times when you need general assistance in using a Windows 98 feature.

Many Help topic windows in Windows 98 Help have a little short-cut button in the text (a button with a curved arrow pointing up and to the left). When you click this button, Windows opens the dialog box or window that's being described in the text so that you can go ahead and make any necessary changes.

Getting the Statistics on a Disk, Folder, or File

You can get quick information about the capacity and amount of free space on a disk by using the Web Page view in the My Computer window. Simply open the My Computer icon on the Windows desktop and then select the icon of the disk drive about which you want information. The statistics on the total capacity, as well as the used and free disk space, then appear in the info panel on the left side of the My Computer window, as you see in the following figure. (If you don't see a My Computer info panel, choose <u>V</u>iew⇨As <u>W</u>eb Page from the My Computer menu bar.)

You can also get this type of information about a diskette, plus information about the size of folders and files on your diskettes, by opening the object's Properties dialog box. Just open a browsing window with the drive, folder, or file that you want the lowdown on and then right-click its icon. Select the Properties command from its shortcut menu.

The following figure shows the (C:) Properties dialog box that appears when I choose to view the properties of my hard drive in the My Computer window.

The (C:) Properties dialog box contains the following tabs and information:

+ **General:** Shows you the name of the disk (or its label, in the case of diskettes), the amount of used and free space on the disk, and the disk's total storage capacity (topped off with a great big pie chart).

+ **Tools:** Contains a Check Now button for checking the disk for errors, a Backup Now button for backing up the contents of the disk with the Microsoft Backup utility, and a Defragment Now button to rearrange the files on the disk in contiguous blocks (*see* "System Tools" in Part IV for more on using these utilities).

+ **Sharing:** Contains options for sharing your drive on a Local Area Network (Shared As and Share Name), setting the type of access (Read-Only, Full, or Depends on Password), setting a password for gaining access (Read-Only Password or Full Access Password, depending on the type of access you choose).

+ **Compression:** Contains a Compress Drive option to compress the contents of the selected drive and a Create New Drive button that you can use to create a new compressed drive, using the free space on the selected drive.

You can also use the Properties command to get information on individual folders and files on your disk. The following figure shows the Properties dialog box displayed for a folder.

The Properties dialog box contains a General tab and, if your computer is on a LAN, a Sharing tab (*see* Sharing in the preceding list for details).

The General tab in a folder's Properties dialog box tells you the location, size in bytes, the number of folders and files contained within the folder, MS-DOS name, creation date, and the folder's attributes which can be Read-only, Archive, Hidden, and System. You can also select the Enable Thumbnail View check box at the bottom of the Properties dialog box to have Windows create a thumbnail image of the contents of graphics and HTML files in the selected folder when you choose <u>V</u>iew⇨Th<u>u</u>mbnails.

The Properties dialog box for a file contains a General tab and, depending on the type of file (document versus program, and the type of document it is), tabs with specific file information. The General tab in a file's Properties dialog box tells you the Windows 98 filename, file type, file's location, size in bytes, DOS filename, creation date, last edited (modified) date, last opened (accessed) date, and the file's attributes which can be Read-only, Archive, Hidden, and System. Please don't fool with the attributes unless you're certain that you know what you're doing.

Installing/Uninstalling Programs

As you continue to use Windows 98, you undoubtedly will get new programs that you need to install on your computer. So too, as time goes on and disk space becomes more precious or newer versions of the software come your way, you may need to uninstall the programs that you added.

Putting those programs on your computer

To install a new program from diskettes or a CD-ROM by using the Add/Remove Programs Control Panel, follow these steps:

1. Click the Start button and then choose <u>S</u>ettings⇨<u>C</u>ontrol Panel to open the Control Panel window.

2. Open the Add/Remove Programs Control Panel to open the Add/Remove Programs Properties dialog box.

3. Put the CD-ROM in your computer's CD-ROM drive or put the first diskette in your computer's floppy disk drive.

4. Click the <u>I</u>nstall button in the Add/Remove Programs Properties dialog box and then click the <u>N</u>ext button. Follow the steps as outlined in the Install Program From Floppy or CD-ROM Installation wizard to install your new program.

You can also use the Run command on the Start menu to install a program from the Run dialog box. In the Open text box in the Run dialog box, you type the drive letter that contains the disk or CD-ROM from which the program will be installed, followed by a colon and the name of the installation program (either **setup** or **install**). For example, to install a new CD-ROM game that uses install as its installation command, you type

d:\install

in the Open text box of the Run dialog box and then click the OK button or press Enter.

Use the Install Wizard to install all new Windows 98 versions of software (also known as 32-bit versions of a program). Install programs from the Run dialog box when you install older software whose installation instructions talk about entering an install or setup command in the Run dialog box.

See also "Add/Remove Programs" in Part IV for more on using this utility.

Taking those programs off your computer

Windows 98 includes an uninstall utility that takes the pain out of removing unneeded or obsolete versions of a program from your computer. To uninstall a program installed with Windows 98 (as described in the preceding section, "Putting those programs on your computer"), follow these steps:

1. Choose Settings⇨Control Panel to open the Control Panel window.

2. Open the Add/Remove Programs control panel to open the Add/Remove Programs Properties dialog box.

3. Select the program to be removed in the list box on the Install/Uninstall tab of the Add/Remove Programs Properties dialog box and then click the Add/Remove button.

4. Click the Yes button in the Confirm File Deletion alert box to begin uninstalling the selected program.

5. To close this dialog box, click the OK button in the Remove Programs From Your Computer dialog box when the message Uninstall successfully completed appears. Then click OK again or click the Close box to close the Add/Remove Programs Properties dialog box.

Use the Windows 98 uninstaller to get rid of any unwanted program that you've installed with the Add/Remove Programs Control Panel. Using this utility to remove a program (rather than just deleting the program's folder) ensures that all vestiges of the program are removed from the system and that you get back every byte of storage space that you're entitled to.

Launching Programs

In Windows 98, you can open the programs that you've installed on your hard drive in any one of the following three ways:

+ **Select the program on the Programs menu, which you open from the Start menu:** *See* "Starting off with the Start Menu" in Part I for information about starting programs from the Start menu and manually adding items to or removing them from the Programs menu.

+ **Open a shortcut to the program or to a document you open regularly:** *See* "Shortcuts" in Part I for information about creating shortcuts for opening a program or a file that in turn opens its associated program.

+ **Open a file created with the program:** *See* "Files" in Part I and "Getting a Preview of a File's Contents" or "Opening Files and Folders" in this part for information about opening a program by opening its file.

You can also launch programs by adding buttons for them to the Quick Launch toolbar on the taskbar and then clicking their buttons. *See* "Calling on the Quick Launch toolbar" in Part I for details.

Moving and Resizing Windows

You can move windows around the desktop and resize them from full-screen (called *maximized*) all the way down to wee buttons on the taskbar (called *minimized*) at your convenience.

To move a window, follow these steps:

1. If necessary, restore the window to an in-between size, either by clicking the Restore Window button if the window is maximized or by clicking its taskbar button if the window is minimized.

2. Position the mouse pointer over the window's title bar.

3. Drag the outline of the window to its new location on the desktop.

4. Release the mouse button to drop the window in its new location on the desktop.

To maximize a window, you have two methods to choose from:

✦ Click the Maximize button on the window's title bar if the window is displayed at less than full size. (The Maximize button is located in the middle of the three buttons on the right side of the title bar.) Otherwise, click the window's taskbar button if the window is minimized.

✦ Choose Maximize from the window's Control menu (which you open by clicking the program's icon in the far left of the window's title bar).

Remember that after you maximize a window, you can restore the window to its original size by doing one of these two things:

✦ Click the Restore button on the window's title bar. (The Restore button is located in the middle of the three buttons on the right side of the title bar.)

✦ Choose Restore from the window's Control menu (which you open by clicking the program's icon in the far left of the window's title bar).

To minimize a window to just a button on the taskbar, you can do either of the following:

✦ Click the Minimize button on the window's title bar. (The Minimize button is the one with the minus sign, located on the left of the three buttons on the right side of the title bar.)

✦ Choose Minimize from the window's Control menu (which you open by clicking the program's icon in the far left of the window's title bar).

In addition to using the automatic sizing controls, you can manually size a window (assuming that it's not currently minimized or maximized) by dragging any of its sides or corners. You can always tell when Windows 98 will allow you to move one or more of the sides of a window by dragging, because the mouse pointer changes from the standard pointer to a double-headed arrow.

Keep the following points in mind to get the most out of resizing windows while you work:

✦ Move a window whenever something else (like the taskbar or another window) gets in the way so that you can't see the window's contents.

✦ Maximize a window when you're doing some serious work (or playing) in that window and don't need the distraction of all the other junk that populates the Windows 98 desktop.

✦ Minimize a window when you still need it open (especially when it's running processes, such as printing or calculating, in the background) but won't be directly using its features for a while.

✦ Keep the window sized in between when you need to see part of its contents on the desktop at the same time you're doing something else (as when moving or copying with drag-and-drop).

See "Dominating the Control Menu" in Part I for information on how to use the Control menu to size and move windows, and *see* "Windows" in Part I to find out about the different parts of windows.

Moving Files and Folders

See "Copying Files and Folders."

Opening Files and Folders

The most common way to open a file or folder is to open its icon in one of the three browsing windows (My Computer, Windows Explorer, or Internet Explorer 4). *See* "Browsing Folders on a Local Disk" in Part II for details.

How you open the file or folder icon after you have it displayed in a browsing window depends on the Active Desktop setting that your computer uses:

✦ Single-click the icon when you've set up the Active Desktop so that icons act and look like hyperlinks (so-called Web style).

✦ Double-click the icon when you've set up the Active Desktop with the so-called "classic" setting (*see* "Changing the way you select and open icons" in Part II for information on changing between Web style and classic style).

Remember that you can also open a file or folder by right-clicking its icon and then choosing the <u>O</u>pen command at the top of its shortcut menu.

See also "Selecting Files and Folders" in this part for information about selecting files and folders after the folder is open.

Playing CDs

With a CD-ROM drive, a sound card, and some cool speakers, you can listen to music while you work, or play great multimedia CD-ROMs, like Myst and Riven, on your lunch hour and breaks.

Today's CD-ROM drives can play audio CDs (compact discs) as well as CD-ROMs with multimedia programs, such as encyclopedias and games, games, games.

To play the latest Counting Crows or Blues Traveler compact disc in your CD-ROM player, follow these steps:

1. Insert the CD (the shiny side with rainbows and no writing) face down in the CD-ROM drive.

2. When you close the door on the CD-ROM drive, Windows reads information that tells it that the CD is of the audio (compact disc) type rather than the data (CD-ROM) type, and then Windows automatically opens the CD Player window (like the one shown in the following figure).

3. To start playing the CD, click the play button (the one with the triangle pointing to the right). To pause the CD, click the pause button (the one with two vertical bars). To stop the CD, click the stop button (the one with the square). To eject the CD, click the eject button (the one with the triangle pointing up, over a single horizontal bar).

TIP

If the CD Player window doesn't automatically open when you pop an audio CD into your CD-ROM drive, click the Start button and then choose Programs➪Accessories➪Multimedia➪CD Player to jump start the window.

Note that you can control the volume for the CD Player (as well as the volume for any of the stuff connected to your sound card) in the Volume Control window. To open this window from the CD Player window, choose View➪Volume Control.

Playing multimedia CD-ROMs

If you place a CD-ROM that has some multimedia program or game into your CD-ROM drive, Windows 98 automatically opens a window showing the folders and files on the drive (D : \ on most computers) instead of opening the CD Player.

If this is the first time you've used the multimedia program, you probably need to install it. If you see a window icon named Install in the D:\ window, open it to install the program. After you install the program, open the program's icon in the D:\ window to start the program or game.

You can play audio CDs in the background while doing other stuff (like writing a letter in your word processor or updating an expense account in your spreadsheet program). Depending on the type of CD-ROM program you have, you may be able to pause the program while you do other stuff in Windows 98. (Some games, however, won't let you pause or save your place, and you may get yourself good and killed if you activate another program window or go to the desktop to do something.)

See also "Multimedia" in Part IV for information about changing the sound and multimedia settings for your computer.

I want my DVD!

Windows 98 supports the new DVD (alternately known as Digital Versatile Disc or Digital Video Disc) computer drives. DVD drives can read both audio CD-ROMs and DVD disks, which currently offer mostly feature-length movies, such as *Face/Off* and *Contact*. To play a DVD disk in your DVD player, you simply pop the disk into your drive and wait for the DVD Player window to open.

If the window doesn't open automatically, you can open it manually: Click the Start button and then choose Programs➪Accessories➪Multimedia➪DVD Player.

After the DVD Player window opens, you can play, pause, stop, and eject the disk by using the same buttons you use when using the CD Player:

+ To start playing the DVD disc, click the play button (the one with the triangle pointing to the right).

+ To pause the DVD disc, click the pause button (the one with two vertical bars).

+ To stop playing the DVD disc, click the stop button (the one with the square).

+ To eject the DVD disc, click the eject button (the one with the triangle pointing up, over a single horizontal bar).

Printing in Windows 98

Although printing is usually performed with a program, such as a word processor or a graphics program, you can print documents directly from the Windows 98 desktop. You simply drag the icon for the file you want to print to the icon for the printer you want the file printed on. Windows then opens the file in the program that created it, while simultaneously sending it to the printer.

You can avoid opening a browsing window containing the icon of the file to be printed and then having to open the Printers window (by choosing Settings⇨Printers on the Windows Start menu) with the icon of the printer: Create a shortcut to the printer on the Windows desktop. That way, to print a file you only have to open the browsing window with the document's file icon and then drag that icon to the printer's shortcut on the desktop (*see* "Shortcuts" in Part II for details on creating a desktop shortcut for your printer).

Managing the print queue

Sometimes after sending a bunch of files to a printer, you find that nothing's getting printed and you need to check out the printer's queue to find out what is or is not going on. Because Windows 98 supports background printing, a printer's queue can get pretty stacked up with print jobs even when everything is proceeding normally.

To check out the print jobs in your printer's queue, you need to follow these steps:

1. Open the My Computer icon on the desktop and then open the Printers window by opening the icon for the Printers folder.

  You can also open the Printers window by choosing Settings⇨Printers from the Start menu.

2. Open the icon for the Printer that contains the print jobs you want to examine.

  Windows opens a window, shown in the following figure, for the printer that you selected (such as Apple LaserWriter NTX or HP LaserJet 4) that shows the documents in the print queue (in the order in which they are to be processed), the status of the print job, the owner of the print job, the progress of the job, and the time at which the job started printing.

  Note that you can also open this window with the print queue by right-clicking the printer's icon in the status area on the Windows taskbar and then selecting the name of the printer from the pop-up menu that appears.

Document Name	Status	Owner	Progress	Started At
Microsoft Word - 02549Pt3	Printing	GREG	0 bytes of 8...	12:56:49 PM 12/30/97
Microsoft Word - 02549toc		GREG	85.2KB	12:56:50 PM 12/30/97
MGE Quarterly Sales.xls		GREG	25.0KB	12:56:50 PM 12/30/97

Apple LaserWriter IIg — Printer Document View Help — 3 jobs in queue

3. After the window with the print jobs queued up for your printer opens, you can do any of the following things to its contents:

- To temporarily pause the printing of the documents in the print queue, choose Printer⇨Pause Printing.

- To remove all the print jobs from the print queue, choose Printer⇨Purge Print Documents.

- To remove a particular file from the print queue, select it in the list and then choose Document⇨Cancel Printing.

- To change the position of a document in the print queue, drag its print queue description to a new position in the list (you can tell where the print job will appear by the appearance of the dark I-beam at the mouse pointer). Note that you cannot move a print job to a new position in the queue if the document's status shows that the job is currently being printing.

4. After you finish reviewing and changing the settings for the jobs in the print queue, click the Close box on the printer's window or choose Printer⇨Close.

If you are printing from a laptop computer or on a desktop computer connected to a LAN, you can use the Print⇨Use Printer Offline command to delay the printing of the files you send to a particular printer.

When you first choose this command to put the printer in off-line mode, all print jobs that you send to the printer are stored in a queue until such time as you choose Print⇨Use Printer Offline again to put the printer back on-line (presumably because the printer is now available to your computer).

Installing a new printer

The day may come when you finally get the boss to spring for that new color laser printer. Before you can use that beauty, however, you have to install it by adding the new printer to your Printers folder, using an Add Printer wizard.

When installing a new printer with the Add Printer wizard, you can choose between adding a local printer (that is, one that is directly cabled to your computer through one of its ports) or a network printer (that is, one that is connected to your LAN with an Ethernet connection, just like your computer is connected to the LAN).

To install a new local printer with the Add Printer wizard, you follow these steps:

1. Open the My Computer icon on the desktop and then open the Printers window by opening the icon for the Printers folder.

You can also open the Printers window by choosing Settings⇨Printers from the Start menu.

2. Open the Add Printer icon in the Printers window to start the Add Printer wizard and then click the Next button or press Enter to display the second Add Printer wizard dialog box.

3. By default, the Add Printer wizard selects the Local Printer radio button, so just click the Next button or press Enter to move on to the third Add Printer wizard dialog box.

4. Select the printer manufacturer in the Manufacturers list box and then select the model of your printer in the Printers list box. If your printer came with its own printer drivers on disk, click the Have Disk button to install those drivers.

5. Click the Next button and then select the port for the printer to use in the Available Ports list box of the next Add Printer wizard dialog box.

6. Click the Next button. Then, if you want, edit the name for the printer in the Printer Name text box in the fourth Add Printer wizard dialog box. If you want to make the printer that you're installing the default printer that is automatically used whenever you print from Windows or from within a Windows program, choose the Yes radio button beneath the heading Do you want your Windows-based programs to use this printer as the default printer?

7. Click the Next button. To print a test page using the newly installed printer, leave the Yes (Recommended) radio button selected beneath the heading Would you like to print a test page? in the fifth and last Add Printer wizard dialog box, where you then click the Finish button or press Enter.

To use the Add Printer wizard to install a printer that is available through your Local Area Network, you follow just slightly different steps:

1. Open the My Computer icon on the desktop and then open the Printers window by opening the icon for the Printers folder.

You can also open the Printers window by choosing Settings⇨Printers from the Start menu.

2. Open the Add Printer icon in the Printers window to start the Add Printer wizard and then click the Next button or press Enter to display the second Add Printer wizard dialog box.

3. Select the Network Printer radio button and then click the Next button or press Enter to move on to the third Add Printer wizard dialog box.

4. Enter the path of the new printer on the network in the Network Path or Queue Name text box. If you want to use this printer to print documents in programs that you run in a DOS window (*see* "Doing DOS Stuff" earlier in this part), choose the Yes radio button beneath the heading Do you print from DOS-based programs?

You can also enter the network path name for the printer by clicking the Browse button and then selecting the printer in the Browse for Printer dialog box. To locate the printer, click the Entire Network icon under Network Neighborhood and then keep expanding (by clicking) any workgroup and drive icons that appear below.

5. Click the Next button and then select the printer manufacturer in the Manufacturers list box. Select the model of your printer in the Printers list box. If your printer came with its own printer drivers on disk, click the Have Disk button to install those drivers.

6. Click the Next button. Then, if you want, edit the name for the printer in the Printer Name text box in the fourth Add Printer wizard dialog box. If you want to make the printer that you're installing the default printer that is automatically used whenever you print from Windows or from within a Windows program, choose the Yes radio button beneath the heading Do you want your Windows-based programs to use this printer as the default printer?

7. Click the Next button. To print a test page using the newly installed printer, leave the Yes (Recommended) radio button selected beneath the heading Would you like to print a test page? in the fifth and last Add Printer wizard dialog box, where you then click the Finish button or press Enter.

After you add a printer to your computer, you can start using it when printing with programs like Word 97 and Excel 97, or when printing from Windows itself.

To switch to a new printer that you haven't designated as the default printer in programs like Word and Excel, you need to open the Print dialog box (choose File⇨Print) and then select the printer's name in the Name drop-down list box.

Printing an HTML file in a browsing window

When browsing Web pages in one of the three browsing windows (My Computer, Windows Explorer, or Internet Explorer 4), you can print the pages that you visit. To print the Web page currently displayed in the browsing window, choose File⇨Print to open the Print dialog box, shown in the following figure.

Note that in addition to the normal printing options, like printer name and number of copies, the Print dialog box for a Web page contains some special print options:

✦ **Print frames:** When a Web page uses frames (individual panes on the Web page, each of which can display a part of a different Web page), choose between the As laid out on the screen (to print the frames on the Web page more or less as they appear in the browsing window), Only the selected frame (to print only the frame that is selected), and the All frames individually (to print the information in each frame on a separate page) radio buttons.

✦ **Print all linked documents:** Select this check box when you want to print all the pages that are linked to the current page that you are printing.

✦ **Print table of links:** Select this check box when you want to print a table that lists all the linked documents in the current document at the end of the print job.

Renaming Files and Folders

You can rename file and folder icons directly in Windows 98 by typing over or editing the existing file or folder name as outlined in these steps:

1. Open a browsing window that contains the folder or file you want to rename.

2. Right-click the file or folder icon and select Rename on its shortcut menu.

3. Type the new name that you want to give the folder (up to 255 characters) or edit the existing name (use the Delete key to remove characters and the ← or → key to move the cursor without deleting characters).

4. When you finish editing the file or folder name, press the Enter key to complete the renaming procedure.

 When the file or folder name is selected for editing, typing anything entirely replaces the current name. If you want to edit the file or folder name rather than replace it, you need to click the insertion point at the place in the name that needs editing before you begin typing.

Selecting Files and Folders

See "Icons" in Part I and "Changing the Folder Options for Windows 98" in Part II.

Shutting Down Windows 98

Windows 98 includes a shut-down procedure that you should follow before you pull the plug on your machine.

To shut down Windows 98 so that you can safely shut off your computer and get home to the kids, follow these steps:

1. Click the Start button and then choose Shut Down from the Start menu to open the Shut Down Windows dialog box.

2. To completely shut down Windows and power down your computer, make sure that the Shut Down radio button is selected and then click the OK button or press Enter.

In addition to the Shut Down option, you can select from the following options in the Shut Down Windows dialog box:

+ **Standby:** Choose this radio button when you want to put your computer into a deep sleep. This mode powers down the computer but maintains the state of your desktop.

+ **Restart:** Choose this radio button when you need to restart the computer (which you often have to do after installing a new piece of hardware or software, for example). You can also use this option in the unlikely event that Windows 98 becomes so screwed up that you need to restart the whole shebang (when, for example, all the colors on the desktop get messed up and go all magenta and green on you).

+ **Restart in MS-DOS mode:** Choose this radio button when you are inexplicably possessed by a need to type some DOS command or to take one last look at that ugly, old DOS prompt.

A couple of notes on using the Shut Down option in the Shut Down Windows dialog box:

+ Windows 98 displays a screen telling you that you can safely turn off the power to your computer. Should you decide that you want to restart the computer at that point, press Ctrl+Alt+Del (the old three-finger salute in DOS!) to restart Windows 98.

+ When your computer is connected to a LAN and someone is currently connected to your computer, Windows 98 displays a warning dialog box indicating that you're about to disconnect one or more people. Choose OK to go ahead and make these folks mad as all get out, or choose Cancel and then find out who's connected and make it his or her responsibility to shut down Windows 98 on your computer after he or she logs off (so that you can go home and get a life).

If you ever restart the computer in MS-DOS mode, you can return to the comfort of Windows 98 by typing **exit** at the DOS prompt.

Switching between Programs

The Windows 98 taskbar makes switching between programs as easy as clicking the button representing the program's window. All you have to do to activate a program and bring its window to the top of your screen display is click the program's button on the taskbar.

Windows old-timers can still use the Alt+Tab shortcut keys first introduced in Windows 3.0 to switch among all open windows. In Windows 98, however, when you press Alt+Tab, a dialog box like the one shown in the following figure appears, with icons for each program window and a description of the icon. When you release both the Alt and Tab keys, Windows activates the window for whatever program icon is selected (indicated by the blue box surrounding the icon).

You can switch to another program that you have open anytime you need to check something in that program or need to get some work done. You also need to switch to a program so that you can close its window (and thereby shut it down) when you no longer need its services but do need the computer memory that the program is hogging.

See also "Taskbar" in Part I for more on doing tricks with the amazing taskbar.

Part IV

Accessories and Control Panel Settings for Every Appetite

The accessories are little extra programs thrown into the Windows 98 operating system that make Windows 98 more versatile, as well as just a bit safer and easier to use. (And hey, as every clothing retailer will tell you: No outfit is complete without a few accessories!)

In addition to giving you those extra utilities in the form of accessories, Windows 98 enables you to customize a whole slew of its settings by fiddling with its many Control Panels. Windows 98 offers Control Panels for doing everything from setting the correct date and time on your computer to specifying your Internet settings so that you can get on the World Wide Web and wait — I mean surf — with everybody else.

In this part . . .

✔ **Computing with the Calculator accessory to find out just how broke you are**

✔ **Changing various and sundry Control Panel settings in your attempt to customize Windows 98**

✔ **Going to the Games accessories to lighten up and have a little fun in life**

✔ **Playing around with the Phone Dialer accessory to call home and explain why you'll be late for the fifth time this week**

✔ **Setting upon the System Tools accessories to make your computer run better**

Accessing Your Accessories

To access any of the many Windows 98 accessories (all of which are covered in this part of the book), click the Start button on the Windows taskbar, choose Programs⇨Accessories, and then click the name of the actual accessory program you want to use on the Accessories menu.

Note that many of the accessories are grouped together in their own categories, which have names like Communications, Entertainment, Fax, Games, System Tools, and the like. To open these programs, highlight the category folder on the Accessories menu, and then highlight and click the particular accessory program icon on the menu that appears.

If you find that some of the accessories covered in this part were not installed on your computer as part of the original Windows 98 installation, you can add them. All you need to do is use the Windows Setup tab on the Add/Remove Programs Properties dialog box, which you open with the Add/Remove Programs Control Panel. (*See* "Control Panel" later in this part for more on the Add/Remove Programs Control Panel.)

Accessibility

The Accessibility folder located at the very top of the Accessories menu contains two utilities that make it easier for people with less-than-perfect physical dexterity to operate a computer. In the Accessibility folder you find:

+ **Accessibility Settings Wizard:** Steps you through configuration settings that determine the smallest size of fonts and other items that appear on-screen.

+ **Microsoft Magnifier:** Makes the screen more readable for the visually impaired. The magnifier creates a separate window that displays a magnified image of a portion of your screen. When you open the utility, the dialog box shown in the figure enables you to determine the necessary degree of magnification; you also use the dialog box to turn the feature on and off.

Calculator

The Calculator accessory, shown in the following figure, supplies you with an on-screen calculator that you can use to perform all sorts of arithmetic computations on the fly.

The following is a list of the buttons found on the calculator and their functions:

- **Numbers 0-9:** To enter a value, click the number buttons or type the number from the keyboard or numeric keypad.

- **CE:** Click to clear an entry.

- **C:** Click to clear the calculator of all entries and calculations.

- **+:** Click after entering a value to add one value to another.

- **–:** Click after entering a value to subtract one value from another.

- ***:** Click after entering a value to multiply one value by another.

- **/:** Click after entering a value to divide one value by another.

Note that the preceding operator buttons (+, –, *, and /) also function as subtotal buttons, enabling you to perform running calculations with mixed operators.

The other calculator buttons and their purposes are as follows:

- **=:** Click to get the total of an addition, subtraction, multiplication, or division calculation.

- **sqrt:** Enter a value, and then click this button to get the square root of that value.

- **MS:** To store a value or the result of a calculation into the calculator's memory, enter the value or perform the calculation and then click this button.

- **M+:** To add a value or calculation to those already stored in the calculator's memory, enter the value or perform the calculation and then click this button.

- **MR:** Click to enter a value stored in the calculator's memory.

- **MC:** Click to clear the calculator's memory.

If you're an engineer and need access to enigmatic functions such as sine, cosine, and tangent, you can switch the simple bank-balance version of the calculator to a fancy-Dan scientific calculator by choosing View⇨Scientific on the menu bar.

Communications

The Communications folder on the Accessories menu contains networking utilities which enable you to connect your computer to other computers on a Local Area Network (LAN), Wide Area Network (WAN), or the Internet and the World Wide Web.

Dial-Up Networking

The Dial-Up Networking accessory enables you to connect to networked computers via modem. For example, if you have a desktop computer at home or a laptop computer on the road that's networked together with your work computer, you use the Dial-Up Networking accessory to access your e-mail or other files on your main PC via your modem. In today's Web-centric computer environment, you also use Dial-Up Networking to access the Internet.

The first time you select the Dial-Up Networking accessory, Windows starts a Welcome to Dial-Up Networking wizard, which walks you through the steps for setting up your computer so that either it can dial into other computers or others can dial into it. After that initial use, you can create additional dial-up connections for other computers with this accessory, either by selecting and opening the Make New Connection icon in the Dial-Up Networking dialog box (shown in the following figure) or by choosing the Make New Connection command from the Connections pull-down menu.

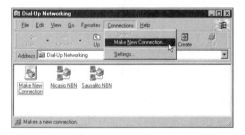

When you set up your computer so that it can dial up another computer or your Internet Service Provider (ISP), you create a connection that contains information about the type of modem on your computer and the name and telephone number of the computer you connect to. You can then use this connection to dial up the other computer by opening the Connections icon in the Dial-Up Networking dialog box and then choosing the Connect button in the Connect To dialog box.

Direct Cable Connection

You use the Direct Cable Connection accessory when you need to connect two computers that are located in the same place but aren't already networked. For example, you can use this accessory to connect a laptop computer to your desktop PC and then copy the data files from the PC to the laptop that you need to take with you on a business trip.

To successfully set up a connection between two computers with the Direct Cable Connection accessory, you need a parallel or serial cable (parallel is faster, if you have it) that reaches between the two machines. If you have a parallel cable, you connect the ends of it to the port marked LPT1 on the back of each computer. If you have a serial cable, connect the ends of it to the port marked either COM1 or COM2 on the back of each computer — but don't you dare connect one end to COM1 and the other to COM2!

When you select the Direct Cable Connection accessory, the Direct Cable Connection wizard shown in the preceding figure walks you through the followings steps for connecting two computers:

1. Choose whether or not the computer you are running this accessory on is the Host or Guest computer. The Host is the computer that contains the data you want to copy to the other. The Guest is the computer to which you want to copy data files.

2. Select the type of cable and port connection (Parallel Cable on LPT1, Serial Cable on COM1, or Serial Cable).

3. Physically connect the cable to the selected type of port on each computer.

4. Click the Finish button to close the Direct Cable Connection wizard. You then need to select the same Direct Cable Connection accessory on the other computer, this time specifying the opposite setting (meaning that you choose Guest if you previously chose Host, or you choose Host if you previously chose Guest).

HyperTerminal

HyperTerminal enables you to connect to a remote computer even if the remote computer isn't running Windows. You can also use HyperTerminal to send and receive files, or to connect to computer bulletin boards and other information programs.

The HyperTerminal window, shown in the following figure, contains the Hypertrm icon, along with icons for other e-mail services, such as CompuServe, AT&T, and MCI Mail.

You open the Hypertrm icon to access the Connection Description dialog box, where you create a dialing connection to the remote computer you want to access. Enter a description for the new connection you are creating, select an icon for it, indicate the telephone number to which the computer's modem is connected, and indicate the port you are connecting to on the remote computer. To connect to the remote computer, simply choose the Dial button in the Connect dialog box that comes up at the end of this process. Thereafter, your new connection icon is available in the HyperTerminal window for future connections.

After connecting to the remote computer, you can send and receive files by using commands on the Transfer menu, or you can use the send/receive buttons on the toolbar in the HyperTerminal window. Likewise, use the commands on the Call menu or the call/disconnect buttons on the toolbar in the HyperTerminal window to make a connection or to terminate the connection when you finish transferring files between the connected computers.

To gain access to files and printers on another computer running Windows, use the Dial-Up Networking accessory rather than HyperTerminal.

Phone Dialer

The Phone Dialer accessory enables you to call all your friends and family from your computer via your modem (even if they aren't in your calling circle).

When you select this accessory, Windows 98 opens the Phone Dialer window, where you can specify the number to call and then have your computer dial it.

 The Phone Dialer contains a neat speed-dial feature that stores up to eight telephone numbers (entered in the Edit Speed Dial dialog box that you access by choosing Edit⇨ Speed Dial). You can dial a number stored on a speed-dial button simply by clicking its button (or pressing Alt plus its speed dial number). In addition to using the speed-dial buttons to enter the phone number to call, you can enter the telephone number in the Number to Dial text box by clicking the digits on the ten-key pad.

One of the great features of the Phone Dialer accessory is that you can specify all the dialing parameters required by your telephone system (which you do from the Dialing Properties dialog box that you open by choosing Tools⇨Dialing Properties [*see* "Control Panel"]). These calling parameters can include stuff like the codes for making outside local calls, codes for making long-distance calls, and even which calling card to use in making toll calls.

Control Panel

The Control Panel in Windows 98 is the place to go when you need to make changes to various settings of your computer system. To open the Control Panel window, do one of the following things:

+ Click the Start button on the taskbar and then choose Settings⇨Control Panel on the Start menu.

+ Open the My Computer window from the Windows desktop and then open the Control Panel folder icon found there.

+ Type **control panel** in the Address bar found at the top of any of the three browsing windows (My Computer, Windows Explorer, and Internet Explorer 4), or type it on the taskbar when you choose Toolbar⇨Address from the taskbar's shortcut menu. Then press Enter.

+ Click the Control Panel icon in the Address bar drop-down menu of the three browsing windows. (Note that this icon appears only in Internet Explorer's drop-down menu when you browse local folders.)

The Control Panel window contains a wide selection of Control Panel icons that you can use to customize the Windows 98 settings on your computer. After you open the Control Panel window open, you can use the mouse to open the icon whose settings you want to change.

The following table lists both the Control Panel icons that you often find in the Control Panel and their uses.

Icon	What It Does
32bit ODBC	The 32 bit ODBC (Open DataBase Connectivity) Properties dialog box enables you to mess around with the data source drivers used in Windows 98. These drivers enable your system to access databases created with all kinds of weird database management software, and they also enable you to add, delete, or configure the locations of those database files on your system (referred to as *data sources*). Not for the faint of heart.
Accessibility Options	The Accessibility Properties dialog box allows you to change a number of keyboard, sound, display, and mouse settings that can make using the computer easier if you have less-than-perfect physical dexterity.

Icon	What It Does
Add New Hardware	The Add New Hardware Properties dialog box opens to a wizard that walks you through the installation of new hardware, such as a new sound card or CD-ROM player. The questions the wizard asks can be pretty technical, so if you're not prepared to supply all the answers, leave this operation to someone more computer savvy; that way, you can blame that person if the installation gets messed up.
Add/Remove Programs	The Add/Remove Programs Properties dialog box enables you to install or uninstall programs on your computer. The Add/Remove Programs Properties dialog box contains three tabs: Install/Uninstall, Windows Setup, and Startup Disk. Use the Install button on the Install/Uninstall tab to add new programs (*see* "Installing/Uninstalling Programs" in Part III for details). Use the check box options on the Windows Setup tab to add components to or remove components from the Windows 98 operating system. Use the Create Disk button on the Startup Disk tab to make an emergency startup floppy disk that you can use to start Windows 98 should the operating system one day decide that it no longer wants to boot for you.
Date/Time	The Date/Time Properties dialog box is where you reset the current date and time. If you live in a region that goes in and out of daylight savings time, you can have Date/Time adjust your computer's clock automatically. Use the Time Zone tab to modify the time zone by selecting the zone from the drop-down list box.
Display	The Display Properties dialog box enables you to customize just about every parameter that affects the way your computer is displayed on a monitor, including the desktop wallpaper, the screen saver, windows color schemes, which Active Desktop items are displayed on the Active Desktop, and the number of colors and the size of the screen area. *See* "Display Properties" in this part for details.
Find Fast	The Find Fast Properties dialog box enables you to create and update various indexes that greatly speed up file searches using specific text or phrases that you perform in Windows 98 or with a Microsoft Office program. *See also* "Finding Files and Folders," in Part III, for information on how to search for files in Windows 98.
Fonts	The Fonts dialog box shows you all the fonts installed on your computer, as well as installs any new fonts you may get your hands on. To add a new font to Windows 98, choose File➪Add New Font and then select the font file in the Add Fonts dialog box.
Game Controllers	The Game Controllers dialog box is where you add and configure the killer joystick or game pad you bought to ensure that you dominate when playing your favorite game.

(continued)

Icon	What It Does
Infrared	The Infrared Monitor dialog box enables you to keep track of your computer's infrared activity. You can find out what infrared devices are within range of your computer, the current infrared communication status, and define what type of infrared activity is allowed and how the Infrared Monitor reports detected infrared activity.
Internet	The Internet Properties dialog box enables you to configure all aspects of your Web-browsing experience. The basic settings include defining a home page for your browser; creating a folder for temporary pages to view offline; clearing your History folder; choosing security levels that restrict content that can potentially damage your computer; defining content that can be viewed in your browser; setting up an Internet connection; and selecting programs for mail, new, and address book. Note that you can also open this dialog box by choosing View⇨Internet Options in the Internet Explorer 4 window. *See Internet Explorer 4 For Windows For Dummies Quick Reference* (published by IDG Books Worldwide, Inc.), by yours truly, for details on configuring all these options.
Keyboard	The Keyboard Properties dialog box adjusts the rate at which characters are repeated when you hold down a key, adjust the cursor blink rate, selects a country and language layout for the keyboard, and changes the type of keyboard (should you add a new keyboard after Windows 98 is installed).
Microsoft Mail Postoffice	The Microsoft Workgroup Postoffice Admin wizard is what your network administrator uses to create or administer a post office location for sending and receiving messages on your LAN.
Modems	The Modems Properties dialog box tells you what modems are installed on your computer, as well as gives you a place to change their dialing properties. The Diagnostics tab of this dialog box is where you find out what COM (communications) port each modem uses.
Mouse	The Mouse Properties dialog box lets you change all kinds of mouse settings, such as setting a right-handed or left-handed button configuration, double-click speed, change which icon is used as the mouse pointer when you're doing different stuff in Windows, modify the speed of the mouse pointer and add or remove mouse trails (that mouse afterimage junk that will drive you nuts in no time at all), and add a new mouse if you get one after installing Windows 98.

Icon	What It Does
Multimedia	The Multimedia Properties dialog box enables you to mess with all sorts of multimedia settings, such as change the playback or recording volume level, the preferred device for recording, or the recording quality for your sound card; add MIDI instruments or select a custom configuration for music produced with MIDI; change the drive designation for a CD-ROM player; change the size of the window in which digital video plays on your computer; display all the multimedia devices currently installed on your computer; and get information about particular devices (and possibly remove them).
Network	The Network dialog box lets your network administrator administer the LAN to his or her heart's content. These settings are not something that you should undertake unaided if you're a network lightweight, even if you consider yourself a Windows wonk.
Passwords	The Passwords Properties dialog box enables the network administrator for your LAN to add or change the password required to use various services on your computer system (like Windows 98 itself), enable remote administration of your computer, standardize all the preferences and Desktop settings, or let individual users create their own profile settings, which determine what icons appear on the Desktop and Start menu. This Control Panel is another one you should be very savvy about before using.
PC Card (PCMCIA)	(Laptop computers only) The PC Card (PCMCIA) Properties dialog box enables you to see all the PC cards that you have inserted into the slots in your laptop computer. You can also stop the use of a particular PC card (so that you can safely remove the card without having to shut down your computer) by selecting the card in the list box and then choosing the Stop button.
Power Management	(Laptop computers only) The Power Management Properties dialog box is where you create individual power schemes for your computer. A *power scheme* is a collection of settings that manage the power usage of your computer and its peripherals (if the peripherals support power management features), thus reducing the power consumption of your computer system. Depending on your hardware, you can let Power Management turn off your monitor and hard disks automatically to save power, put the computer on standby when it is idle (particularly useful for conserving battery power in portable computers), or put your computer in hibernation, which is a deeper sleep mode that preserves your desktop and restores it to its previous state when you wake up your computer.

(continued)

Icon	*What It Does*
Printers	The Printers dialog box shows you all the printers that are currently installed for use on your computer (or your workgroup, if you are on a network) and enables you to add a new printer. *See* "Installing a new printer" in Part III for details.
QuickFinder Manager	The QuickFinder Manager dialog box lets you create, edit, delete, or update a Fast Search. You can also use the options in this dialog box to see Fast Search information, specify Fast Search preferences, determine how QuickFinder components are accessed, and perform searches from QuickFinder Manager.
Regional Settings	The Regional Settings Properties dialog box enables you to change the formatting for numbers, currency, dates, and times to suit schemes preferred by countries other than the U.S. This dialog box allows you to select the language and country to be used as the basis for all regional settings.
Sounds	The Sounds Properties dialog box is where you select various sound files to be played when certain events take place (for example, starting Windows 98, opening a new program, maximizing a window, or exiting Windows 98). You can also select from an assortment of sound schemes that are already matched to specific Windows 98 events.
System	The System Properties dialog box enables you to get system information about your computer, as well as fool around with a lot of settings, such as removing devices (a definite no-no), setting up virtual memory (and if you don't know what that is, you don't need to be setting it) and specifying how much disk space to allocate to it, and optimizing the file systems (especially for use with older, 16-bit application programs).
Telephony	The Dialing Properties dialog box is where you configure modem dialing settings when you make calls from different locations. You can specify country codes, area codes, disable or enable call waiting, enter calling card information, and add or remove telephone drivers. *See* the "Phone Dialer" and "Dial-Up Networking" accessories in this part for more information.
Users	The User Settings dialog box enables you to set up a personal profile that makes preferred desktop settings (background, desktop icons, mouse settings, and so on) available to each person who works on the same computer. To define a username and password so that multiple users can log on to the same computer, use the Add User wizard that appears when you choose the New User button.

Display Properties

The Display Properties dialog box, which you open via the Display Control Panel in Windows 98, has many new features that allow you to customize nearly every aspect of the way the Windows desktop is displayed on your computer.

When you open the Display icon in the Control Panel, you see the preceding Display Properties dialog box. Use the seven tabs in that dialog box to change the following display settings:

◆ **Background tab:** Select a graphics image or HTML (Web page) document to change the pattern or wallpaper used by the desktop. (You change the color of the desktop with the Appearance tab, described in this list.)

◆ **Screen Saver tab:** Select and configure a screen saver and set the interval after which it kicks in. If you have one of those new energy-saving monitors, you can set the interval after which the monitor goes to lower-power standby or shuts off. (If you have such a monitor but Windows 98 isn't using its energy-saving features, first choose the Advanced button on the Settings tab. Then check the Monitor is Energy Star Compliant check box on the Monitor tab of the Display Type dialog box.)

◆ **Appearance tab:** Change the color scheme used by various parts of a window (*see* "Windows" in Part I for the lowdown on the parts) and the color of the desktop. If you change the appearance of an item that uses a font (such as the Icon Title, Inactive Title Bar, or ToolTip), you can change the font and its color, size, and attributes as well.

✦ **Effects tab:** Assign new icons to desktop icons (or restore to the default), select large icons for the desktop and all windows, and choose to display icons in all possible colors. You can also browse to select an icon from another icon file.

✦ **Web tab:** List the channels that you are currently subscribed to as well as the available Active Desktop items. Use the check boxes to select the item to appear on the desktop when using the View as Web Page option for the desktop. This tab also enables you to go to the Folder Options dialog box for further customizations. *See* "Activating/Deactivating the Active Desktop" and "Changing the Folder Options for Windows 98" in Part II for details on using these Web integration features.

✦ **Settings tab:** Change the color palette (meaning the number of colors, such as 16, 256, or even — with some really fancy cards and monitors — millions) used by Windows 98, and resize the desktop area (the higher the number of pixels you select, the smaller the items and fonts appear on the desktop, although making them smaller does allow you to cram more stuff on-screen). You can also use this tab to specify the kind of monitor you have if Windows 98 did not pick up on the monitor type when you first installed it or if you add a new monitor after Windows 98 was installed. If the monitor is Energy Star compliant, define it as such in the Advanced dialog box so that you can take advantage of these energy-saving features. *See* "Power Management."

Entertainment

The Entertainment accessories folder contains utilities that keep you merrily plunking away at the computer long after any actual work is finished and when you should be off somewhere having a life. Keep in mind that to make all this entertainment possible, your computer needs to be equipped with a CD-ROM drive, a sound card, external speakers, and a microphone, among other things.

The Entertainment folder contains the following accessories:

✦ **CD Player:** Lets you play an audio CD (compact disc) in your computer's CD-ROM drive.

✦ **DVD Player:** Lets you play a DVD (Digital Video Disc or Digital Versatile Disc) if you have a DVD disk drive installed in your computer.

✦ **Interactive CD Sampler:** Lets you view interactive, multimedia presentations of Microsoft products; requires the Windows 98 CD-ROM.

✦ **Media Player:** Lets you play audio, video, or animation files, as well as control the settings for multimedia hardware devices.

✦ **Sound Recorder:** Lets you record on disk with a microphone connected to your sound card.

✦ **Trial Programs:** Lets you install a variety of trial programs that run the gamut from money management to edutainment, all brought to you by Microsoft and DreamWorks Interactive.

✦ **Volume Control:** Lets you set the volume and balance for your speakers when playing audio CDs or system sounds or when recording with your microphone.

✦ **WebTV Viewer:** Lets you view standard and specially enhanced television broadcasts (like Internet broadcasts or corporate videos over your company's intranet) and use a configurable on-screen program guide. To receive television broadcasts, your computer must have a TV tuner card. *See* "Viewing TV Channels" in Part II for information on using Microsoft WebTV for Windows in Windows 98.

Games

Because all work and no play makes you a very dull employee, the Games accessory folder in Windows 98 includes the following games to help you while away the hours:

✦ **FreeCell:** A card game that is a lot like the Solitaire game included in earlier versions of Windows. It differs from Solitaire, however, in that all the cards in FreeCell are always face up.

✦ **Hearts:** A great version of the card game we all know and love.

✦ **Minesweeper:** The same game of marking mines that Microsoft gave you in earlier versions of Windows.

✦ **Solitaire:** The old standby game of Solitaire first included in Windows 3.0 and 3.1.

If you need information about how to play the game that you've opened, choose Help➪Help Topics on the game's menu bar.

If your computer is part of a Local Area Network, you can play Hearts with your coworkers on the network by entering your name in the What is your name? text box and choosing the I want to connect to another game radio button in the Microsoft Hearts Network dialog box that appears when you start the Hearts game.

Imaging

The Kodak Imaging accessory is a handy utility that enables you to view and perform basic editing tasks on bitmapped image documents as well as on fax documents and scanned images. You can also annotate the image with a variety of tools. The following figure shows the Imaging window and its optional toolbars — a dinosaur clip art document is open in the editing window.

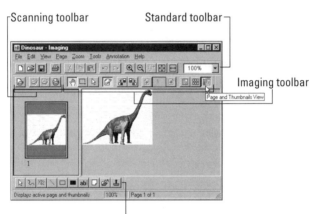

To hide or display a given toolbar, right-click a toolbar and select or deselect the toolbar from the shortcut menu.

The Imaging toolbars offer the following tools:

✦ **Standard:** In addition to the standard open, save, print, cut, copy, and paste buttons, you get zoom options and tools for making the image fit the editing window.

✦ **Scanning:** These tools are for scanning and rescanning an image and give you the capability to insert or append a scanned image.

✦ **Imaging:** These tools are for dragging, selecting, and rotating an image, displaying the annotation toolbar, and changing the view in the editing window to one of three choices: one page, thumbnails of all open images, or a combination of thumbnails and the current image page.

♦ **Annotation:** These tools are for adding graphic and text annotations. Graphics tools include freehand or straight line tools and hollow or filled rectangles. You can highlight text that is either typed in or brought in from another file, as well as attach a note you create or rubber stamp the image with epithets such as Approved, DRAFT, Received, and Rejected.

Multimedia

The Multimedia accessory includes the ActiveMovie Control command for playing movies, sounds, and other multimedia files on your computer's hard drive, on a drive on your Local Area Network, on your company's intranet, or on the World Wide Web.

Notepad

The Notepad accessory offers a simple text file editor that you can use to read, edit, and print text files (such as those last-minute README files that seem to accompany all your software).

In the following figure, you see the resulting Notepad accessory document after I started waxing philosophical with my favorite German philosopher.

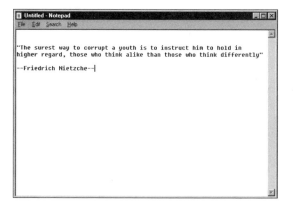

Notes about using the Notepad accessory:

✦ Text files composed in Notepad use a standard, bold Arial font with very simple formatting. (You can't change fonts or attributes or automatically center text, or any of that good stuff, in Notepad.)

✦ Use Notepad to compose files whenever you know that the document must be saved in a true ASCII-type text file or whenever you're not sure that the recipient's computer is equipped with a word processor capable of opening and reading a file that's been truly word-processed, such as with Word or WordPad (*see* "WordPad" later in this part for details).

✦ Notepad is not your typical word processor; if you don't press Enter to start a new line or paragraph when typing, it just keeps on going, and going, and going. Notepad does this because it is first and foremost a text editor for editing programming files, where carriage returns signify a new line of code.

✦ When a file sports the spiral-bound notebook icon, you can tell that it has been saved as a Notepad file and will automatically open Notepad when you open the icon.

Paint

The Paint accessory offers a simple drawing program with which you can create original graphics or edit bitmapped graphics that you get with Windows 98 or other Windows-based programs.

In the following figure, you see the Paint accessory after I used it to whip up a self-portrait.

When you select the Paint accessory, Windows opens an empty Paint window that contains a palette of artist tools on the left side and a palette of colors to choose from on the bottom.

To open a bitmap file with an existing graphic to edit, choose File⇨Open and then designate the filename. To create your own original masterpiece, select a drawing tool and have at it!

You can use the Paint accessory to create your own wallpaper designs for the desktop. Just follow these simple steps:

1. After you finish drawing a new graphic or editing an existing one, save it by choosing File⇨Save.

   If necessary, give your new creation a filename.

2. Choose File⇨ Set As Wallpaper (Tiled) or File⇨Set As Wallpaper (Centered) from the menu bar. (Choose the Tiled command if you're working with a less-than-full-screen picture and want Windows to replicate it so that it fills the entire screen.)

As soon as you select one of these Set As Wallpaper commands, Windows 98 immediately makes your wonderful artwork the backdrop against which all further Windows actions take place.

System Tools

The System Tools accessory comprises a bunch (and I mean a *bunch*) of utilities for keeping your computer system in tip-top shape.

In the System Tools Accessories folder you find the following powerful utilities, which go a long way toward letting you spend quality time with your computer:

✦ **Backup:** Enables you to make, compare, or restore backup copies of particular files and folders on either diskettes or tape. Use this utility to maintain copies of all the files you can't live without, in case (knock on wood) anything ever happens to your computer or its hard drive.

✦ **Character Map:** Lets you copy any character in a particular font (including those symbols and dingbats you can't insert directly from the keyboard) into the Clipboard.

✦ **Clipboard Viewer:** Opens a window that shows you the current contents of the Windows Clipboard.

✦ **Compression Agent:** Saves disk space by compressing selected files, using the settings you specify.

✦ **Disk Cleanup:** Saves disk space by locating unnecessary files, which you can select for deletion.

✦ **Disk Converter (FAT32):** Creates more space on your hard drive by converting file system clusters on your hard drive from FAT16 to smaller FAT32 clusters, thus decreasing the amount of hard drive space a file takes up.

✦ **Disk Defragmenter:** Defragments your hard disk, which means that your files are rearranged so that they use contiguous blocks. This process usually speeds up your computer considerably and is necessary if you use the Media Player.

✦ **DriveSpace:** Compresses your hard drive files to increase storage space.

✦ **Maintenance Wizard:** Helps keep your Windows 98 system in top running condition by using a suite of utilities that increase performance. *See* "Tuning up the old system" later in this part for details.

✦ **Net Watcher:** Enables you to view all the connections currently made to your computer on the LAN, as well as add or stop sharing folders with other users on the network.

✦ **Resource Meter:** Monitors the system resources used by the various programs that you are currently running. Note that using this accessory can make your computer run more slowly.

✦ **ScanDisk:** Checks your diskettes or hard drive for errors and, if possible, fixes the errors that it finds.

✦ **Scheduled Tasks:** Task Scheduler is a tool that runs in the background every time you start Windows. The Scheduled Tasks accessory enables you to schedule tasks (such as run Disk Defragmenter) daily, weekly, monthly, or at certain times, such as in the middle of the night, when your computer is idle. You can change the schedule for or turn off an existing task and customize how a task will run at its scheduled time. *See* "Tasks right on schedule" later in this entry to discover how to get these things done.

✦ **System Information:** Tells you everything you ever wanted to know (and even some things you didn't) about your computer system.

✦ **System Monitor:** Enables you to view all kinds of charts that plot various aspects of the computer system's performance. You can chart data for all sorts of junk you probably couldn't care less about, such as Kernal Threads, the number of IPX packets lost per second, and the percentage of Dirty Data in the 32-bit file system.

◆ **Welcome to Windows:** Opens an interactive tour of the world of Windows 98. *See* "Welcome to Windows" later in this part for more about this tour.

Copying characters from the Character Map

The Character Map System Tools accessory enables you to copy any character in a particular font (including those symbols and dingbats you can't insert directly from the keyboard) into the Clipboard. From there, you can insert the character into your current text file.

To copy characters to and from the Clipboard by using the Character Map accessory, choose Programs⊅Accessories⊅ Character Map on the Start menu to open the Character Map dialog box (see the following figure). Then follow these steps:

1. Choose the font containing the character or characters you want to copy in the Font drop-down list box of the Character Map dialog box. The available characters in the chosen font appear in the viewing area of the dialog box.

2. Select the characters in the font that you want to copy to the Clipboard by double-clicking them or by clicking them and then clicking the Select button. (To display a larger version of a particular character, keep the mouse button pressed after clicking it.)

3. Click the Copy button to actually copy the selected characters (now proudly displayed in the Characters to Copy edit box) to the Clipboard.

4. Switch to the program containing the open text file where you want the copied characters to appear (*see* "Switching between Programs" in Part III of this book if you've never done this before).

5. Position the insertion point at the place in the document text where the copied characters are to be inserted and then choose Edit⊅Paste from the menu bar or press Ctrl+V.

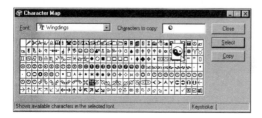

In Windows 98, the Character Map accessory enables you to insert a character from any font into document text regardless of the font chosen for that document. This means that your Wingdings font character chosen in the Character Map dialog box won't turn to its Times New Roman equivalent when you insert it into a text block formatted with the Times New Roman font.

Clipboard Viewer

The Clipboard Viewer System Tools accessory enables you to view the content of the Clipboard. On the surface, this capability doesn't seem like an earth-shattering feature — until you realize that the Clipboard stores its contents in multiple formats, enabling you to transfer information between programs that use different formats. The Display menu in the Clipboard Viewer window lists all the formats available for the information currently on the Clipboard. Just choose the file format of the program you want to copy to, and then complete the copy procedure in that program.

Tasks right on schedule

The Scheduled Tasks System Tools accessory starts each time you crank up Windows 98, where it dutifully runs in the background. When the Scheduled Tasks utility is running, a tiny icon of a window with a red clock appears next to the real clock on the taskbar.

Double-clicking the Scheduled Tasks icon on the taskbar or choosing Programs⇨Accessories⇨System Tools⇨Scheduled Tasks on the Start menu opens the Scheduled Tasks window shown here. You can also open the Scheduled Tasks window by opening the My Computer icon and then opening the Scheduled Tasks folder icon located within.

Name	Schedule	Next Run Time	Last Run Time	Status
Add Scheduled Task				
DTV Loader	Every 3 hour(s) from ...	12:00:00 AM ...	5:59:58 PM 1...	
StarSight Loader	Every 1439 minute(s)...	1:59:00 AM 1...	1:59:59 AM 1...	
Tune-up Defragment programs	At 10:00 AM on 12/...	Never	Never	
Tune-up Disk Cleanup	At 9:15 AM on 12/8/...	Never	Never	
Tune-up Scandisk	At 9:30 AM on 12/8/...	Never	Never	

1 object(s) selected

To schedule a task in the Scheduled Tasks window with the Scheduled Task wizard, follow these steps:

1. In the list of tasks, click the Add Scheduled Task hyperlink to open the first dialog box of Scheduled Task wizard.

2. Click the Next button or press Enter to display the second dialog box of the Scheduled Task wizard, where you select the program to run.

3. In the list box, click the name of the program you want scheduled to run, and then choose the Next button or press Enter to open the third dialog box, where you indicate how often the task should be performed.

4. If you want, enter your own name for the scheduled task in the text box at the top of the dialog box, and then select the radio button (Daily, Weekly, Monthly, One time only, When my computer starts, or When I log on) indicating when you want the task automatically performed. Then click the Next button or press Enter to display the fourth dialog box of the wizard, where you select the start time and date for the scheduled task.

5. Enter a beginning time in the Start time text box or select the time with the spinner buttons, and then designate a starting date in the Start date text box or select it from the drop-down list. Click the Next button or press Enter to display the last dialog box of the Scheduled Task wizard.

6. If you want to further configure your scheduled task, select the Open advanced properties for this task when I click Finish check box before you click the Finish button or press Enter. If you don't need to use the advanced options, just click the Finish button or press Enter without selecting this check box.

When you select the Open Advanced Properties for this task when I click finish check box in the last dialog box of the Scheduled Task wizard, Windows opens a Properties dialog box for the selected task. This Properties dialog box contains three tabs, which have the following options:

✦ **Task:** Use the options on the Task tab to change the program file to be executed by typing its pathname in the Run text box or by browsing to the program file's location on your computer or LAN.

◆ **Schedule:** Use the options on the Schedule tab to change the time and date for a task and to access options to further refine the task schedule.

◆ **Settings:** Use the options on the Settings tab to define settings for the task upon completion, during idle time, and when power management is a consideration (when using a laptop).

Note that you can access the advanced properties for a task at any time after scheduling it by right-clicking the task in the Scheduled Tasks window and then choosing Properties from the shortcut menu.

Also, you can remove a scheduled task by right-clicking the task in the Scheduled Tasks window and then choosing Delete from its shortcut menu and Yes in the alert box asking you to confirm the task's removal to the Recycle Bin.

Make sure that the system date and time for your computer are accurate. The Scheduled Tasks utility relies on this information to know when to run tasks that you schedule.

Tuning up the old system

The Maintenance Wizard accessory (shown in the following figure) helps optimize your computer's performance by routinely doing the following:

◆ Speeding up the performance of frequently used programs

◆ Checking your hard drive for errors with ScanDisk

◆ Freeing up hard drive space by deleting all unnecessary files

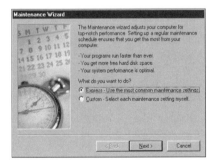

When you choose Windows Tune-Up on the System Tools Accessories menu, the first dialog box of the Maintenance Wizard appears, where you then follow these steps:

1. By default, the Maintenance Wizard selects the Express – Use the most common tune-up settings radio button. To customize the tune-up settings, choose the Custom – Select each tune-up setting myself radio button. Then click the Next button or press Enter to open the second dialog box of the Maintenance Wizard.

2. In the second dialog box of the Maintenance Wizard, select the radio button (Nights – Midnight to 3:00 AM, Days – Noon to 3:00 PM, or Evenings – 8:00 PM to 11:00 PM) that represents the tune-up schedule you want the Windows Tune-Up utility to use. Then click the Next button or press Enter to open the third dialog box of the Windows Tune-Up wizard.

Note that if you selected the Custom – Select each tune-up setting myself radio button in the first dialog box, the second dialog box contains a Custom – Use current settings radio button in addition to the other three regular radio buttons.

The options in the third dialog box depend on whether you selected the Express – Use the most common tune-up settings or the Custom – Select each tune-up setting myself radio button in the first dialog box. If you chose the Express option, the final dialog box appears, and it lists the tune-ups to be performed and their scheduled times. If you chose the Custom option, the dialog box enables you individually to select the programs that automatically open each time Windows starts.

3. In the third dialog box of the Express Maintenance Wizard, click the Finish button. Select the check box labeled When I click Finish, perform each scheduled tune-up for the first time if you want the three tune-up tasks listed in the dialog box performed on your computer as soon as you close the Maintenance Wizard by clicking the Finish button.

In the third dialog box of the Custom Maintenance Wizard, put a check mark in the check boxes of all programs that you want Windows to open automatically when it starts, and remove check marks from the check boxes of programs that you don't want opened. Then click the Next button or press Enter to open the fourth dialog box of the Maintenance Wizard.

4. (Custom only) In the fourth dialog box, by default, the Custom
Maintenance Wizard selects the radio button labeled Yes,
speed up my programs regularly. If you don't want Windows to
speed up your often-used programs by rearranging them on
your hard drive with Disk Defragmenter, choose No, do not
speed up my programs. Then click the Next button or press
Enter to open the fifth dialog box of the Wizard.

Note that when you use the Yes, speed up my programs
regularly option, you can modify when the Disk Defragmenter
rearranges your programs by clicking the Reschedule button
and then selecting the day and time to do this in the Reschedule
dialog box. To customize what drives are defragmented,
click the Settings button and then select which disk
drives to use in the Scheduled Settings for Disk Defragmenter
dialog box.

5. (Custom only) In the fifth dialog box, by default, the Wizard
selects the Yes, scan my hard drive for errors regularly radio
button. If you don't want Windows automatically to scan the
folders and files on your hard drive with its ScanDisk utility,
choose the No, do not scan my hard disk for errors. Then click
the Next button or press Enter to open the sixth dialog box of
the Wizard.

Note that when using the Yes, scan my hard disk for errors
regularly option, you can modify when ScanDisk runs by
clicking the Reschedule button and then selecting the day and
time to do this in the Reschedule dialog box. To customize
what drives are scanned, click the Settings button, and then
select which disk drives to use in the Scheduled Settings for
ScanDisk dialog box.

6. (Custom only) In the sixth dialog box, by default, the Wizard
selects the Yes, delete unnecessary files regularly radio
button. If you don't want Windows to delete files from your
hard drive automatically, choose the No, do not delete
unnecessary files. Then click the Next button or press Enter to
open the seventh (and final) dialog box of the Wizard.

Note that when using the Yes, delete unnecessary files
regularly option, you can modify when the files are deleted by
clicking the Reschedule button and then selecting the day and
time to do this in the Reschedule dialog box. To customize
what types of files are deleted, click the Settings button, and
then, in the Disk Cleanup Settings dialog box, put check marks
in the check boxes of all the types of files you want routinely
deleted, and remove check marks from the types you don't
want routinely deleted.

7. In the seventh dialog box of the Wizard, click the Finish button. Select the check box labeled <u>W</u>hen I click finish, perform each scheduled tune-up for the first time if you want the custom tune-up tasks listed in the dialog box performed on your computer as soon as you close the Maintenance Wizard. Then click the Finish button.

Remember that your computer must be turned on during the times your various tune-up tasks are scheduled to run.

Welcome to Windows

The Welcome to Windows System Tools accessory offers an interactive guided tour of all the new features of Windows 98. When you choose Welcome to Windows on the System Tools Accessories menu, a Welcome to Windows 98 window opens, which has the following options:

✦ **Registration Now:** Click this option to open a Microsoft Windows 98 Registration wizard that walks you through the steps to register Windows 98 online with your modem.

✦ **Connect to the Internet:** Opens the Internet Connection Wizard that takes you through the steps of finding an Internet Service Provider (ISP) and connecting to the Internet for the first time.

✦ **Discover Windows 98:** Click this option to open an interactive tour that shows you all the ins and outs of Windows 98, including new features and a Computer Essentials section for computer newbies.

✦ **Maintain Your Computer:** Click this option to open the Maintenance Wizard. *See* the preceding section, "Tuning up the old system," for details on how to schedule different types of tune-up tasks with this wizard.

After you finish exploring the options in the Welcome to Windows 98 window, click the window's Close box.

When you click the Close box, a Welcome to Windows 98 dialog box opens, asking you if you want Windows to automatically open Welcome to Windows 98 each time you start your computer. Click the <u>N</u>o button if you don't want the Welcome to Windows 98 window in your face each time you start computer. Click the <u>Y</u>es button if, for some strange reason, you decide you want this window to welcome you each time you fire up your computer.

WordPad

WordPad is a kind of "poor man's" Microsoft Word, offering you basic document editing and formatting capabilities and compatibility with documents created with the real Microsoft Word.

The following figure shows the WordPad accessory after I started using it to write my new novel, *Alice in Windowsland.*

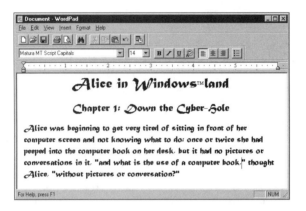

Although it's not nearly as full-featured as Microsoft Word, WordPad is certainly head and shoulders above the Notepad text editor, because WordPad enables you to change fonts and attributes and to format the text with justification or bullets. In fact, WordPad is so sophisticated that you can even preview how pages in the document will print. You access this print preview feature by choosing File⇨Print Preview (or by clicking the Print Preview button on the toolbar — the one with the magnifying glass).

Note that WordPad automatically *saves* its documents in the Word 6 file format, meaning that Word 6 can open any document created with WordPad. However, WordPad can *open* Word documents created in version 6 *or later,* including Word 97. Of course, if you open a document in a folder or on the desktop that was created in WordPad but saved in the Word 6 file format, Windows 98 naturally tries to open Microsoft Word rather than the WordPad accessory, provided that Word 6 is installed on your computer.

Techie Talk

accessories: Tiny (by Microsoft standards) auxiliary programs invented for Windows 98 that aren't really necessary to run your computer but can be really handy.

Active Channels: See *channels*.

Active Desktop: What you get when you enable Web functionality on the desktop. You can turn the Active Desktop on and off by right-clicking anywhere on the desktop and choosing Active Desktop⇔View as Web page.

Active Desktop item: Any World Wide Web component placed directly on your desktop for easy access. Active Desktop items can include miniviews of Web channels (such as the MSN stock ticker), actual Web pages, or special applets (such as the 3D Java clock). Like channels, the contents of Active Desktop items can be routinely updated on a schedule of your choosing.

applications: A techie way of saying "programs" — you know, the things that make your computer run around the room and jump through hoops.

browsing offline: When you are not connected to the Internet and you use a browser (like Internet Explorer 4) to browse Web pages or e-mail and newsgroup messages that have been downloaded onto your own computer. With the advent of Web channels and Web page subscriptions, you can have new content automatically downloaded during the wee hours of the night, when you're not bothered by Internet traffic and lengthy downloads. You can then view the downloads offline at your leisure.

channels: A special content delivery system that enables you to subscribe to specially formatted World Wide Web content. Subscribing to a channel means having fresh, new content brought to you on a regular basis, rather than having to go out Web surfing to find it yourself. Also known as *Active Channels.*

Clipboard: The place in your system memory where items you want to cut or copy from one place to another are stored. The Clipboard holds only one item at a time, and you can see the current Clipboard contents by using the Clipboard Viewer accessory.

context menu: See *shortcut menu.*

Control menu: A pull-down menu attached to every window in Windows 98 that contains the same old tired commands, which you use to resize, relocate, or close the window (just in case you can't adapt to the way Windows 98 performs these functions, or you really miss this feature from Windows 3.1). The Control menu appears as a small version of the program's icon in the top left corner of the program's window.

Control Panel: A window full of icons that enable you to customize the many Windows 98 settings available for your computer.

desktop: The basic background for the Windows 98 environment that contains the taskbar and shortcuts to programs and files that you use. The desktop is the place from which you start and end your work session with a Windows computer.

dialog box: A special, limited type of window that contains any number of buttons, boxes, tabs, and sliders, which you use to specify a whole bunch of settings all at once in Windows 98 or in any other particular Windows program you have open.

DOS: An acronym for (choose one) Disk, Damned, Diabolical, Dumb (our favorite) Operating System. DOS is almost irrelevant with the advent of Windows 98. You can, however, open a window on DOS and have a look-see at your CONFIG.SYS file within Windows 98 if you really miss that kind of stuff!

Explorer: Introduced in Windows 95, Windows Explorer enables you to view the folders, files, disk drives, CD-ROM drives, network drives, and who-knows-what-else that's part of your computer system.

filename: The name you give your files, silly. We're only bringing it up here because Windows 98 allows users to name their files and folders with up to 255 characters, including spaces. Imagine that.

folder: A data container that holds files, other folders, or a combination of the two. Folders used to be called *directories,* even though their icons looked like folders.

HTML (HyperText Markup Language): The traditional computer programming language for the Web (traditional since 1989 – 1990, when the World Wide Web and HTML language first began to make themselves a presence in the world). HTML can run on almost any computer platform, and can combine text with pictures, sounds, and other multimedia enhancements.

HTML document: See *Web page.*

hyperlink: Text or graphics images that you click with the mouse to take you to a certain Web destination (or, rather, have that Web destination appear in your browser window). You can spot a hyperlink when the mouse pointer changes to an outline of a hand. Also, words or other text hyperlinks are almost always underlined text and in blue — which, after you follow the link, changes to purple.

hypertext: Text to which a hyperlink is attached.

icon: A small picture used in Windows 98 to make your computer a more GUI (*gooey,* as in *Graphical User Interface*) place to be. Icons identify all manner of objects associated with your computer.

Internet: A large number of computers of all types all hooked together all around the World. The popular multimedia part of the Internet is the World Wide Web.

intranet: A small-scale version of the Internet that works the same way as the Internet, but only the authorized members of the corporation or organization that sponsors the intranet get to use it.

MSN/Microsoft Network: Enables all the users of Windows 98 to join together throughout the world in an atmosphere of Aquarian goodwill and brotherhood — or just send and receive e-mail, get online help about Windows software, and participate in discussion forums. You can also access various services and — guess what? — SURF THE NET!

multimedia: Yeah! It's what we want: music, color, sound — all the stuff that separates the World Wide Web from just plain text on a monochrome screen. All sorts of sounds and images can be experienced with a properly equipped multimedia computer. Much of the popularity of the Web is based on the visual and audio impact of multimedia.

properties: A description of the settings of any object in Windows 98 that is represented by an icon. Properties are found in special dialog boxes that you access through the object's shortcut menu.

Recycle Bin: The trash can of Windows 98, where you can drag the files, directories, and other stuff that you want to get rid of. Somebody at Microsoft was positively gushing with political correctness when he or she named this thing, because nobody is going to drive up, take the stuff you throw away, and make something wonderful and new with it.

shortcut: A remarkable way in Windows 98 to open a favorite document, folder, or program directly from the desktop of your computer without needing to know its real whereabouts.

shortcut menu: A pull-down menu containing commands that relate directly to the object to which they are attached. Shortcut menus can be found almost everywhere in Windows 98. They're attached to program, folder, or file icons, toolbar buttons, open windows, and even the desktop itself. To open a shortcut menu, right-click the object in question with the mouse. Sometimes known as a *context menu*.

Start menu: The mother of all pull-down menus in Windows 98. Located by clicking the ever-present Start button on the taskbar, it contains almost all the commands you'll ever need to use.

taskbar: A bar that contains buttons for opening the Start menu and switching between programs and windows that are currently in use.

toolbar: A bar containing a row of buttons that perform many of the routine tasks you used to have to do with pull-down menus or keystroke combinations in "the old days."

ToolTips: Windows 98 extensively uses ToolTips to provide a way of adding commentary or footnotes to features. When you run your mouse pointer over a certain part of the screen, a little black-outlined, pale-yellow rectangle pops up with some more or less informative text. In some cases, such as with some Internet search results, this text can amount to a paragraph's worth of context-sensitive material.

View menu: Located in the menu bar, the View menu enables you to modify in various ways the look and feel of all those icons that are going forth and multiplying in your windows.

Web browser: A program such as Microsoft Internet Explorer 4.0 or Netscape Navigator, which enables the user or client to visit various Web sites and experience the content found there. The Internet Explorer 4.0 Web browser also opens files on the same computer on which it is running and displays the local files as Web files.

Web Integrated Desktop: The new technology for extending Web functionality to your computer in the most intimately possible way: by combining certain features of the browser with the Windows 98 operating system itself.

Web page: The basic display unit of the World Wide Web: When you see something on the Internet, it is most likely a Web page. The Web page itself may be composed of a number of parts, including the HTML source and various multimedia images.

Web view: Refers to the special view wherein folder and file icons behave like hyperlinks and HTML documents with related information automatically appear when you hover the mouse over certain customized folder icons.

window: The basic on-screen box used in Windows 98 to contain and display each and every program you run on your computer.

wizards: A particular set of dialog boxes used in Windows 98 and other Microsoft products to step the user through complex procedures, such as installing a new printer, sending a fax, or performing coronary angioplasty.

Index

Notes

Notes

Notes

Notes

Notes

Notes

Notes

Discover Dummies™ Online!

The Dummies Web Site is your fun and friendly online resource for the latest information about ...For Dummies® books on all your favorite topics. From cars to computers, wine to Windows, and investing to the Internet, we've got a shelf full of ...For Dummies books waiting for you!

Ten Fun and Useful Things You Can Do at www.dummies.com

1. Register this book and win!
2. Find and buy the ...For Dummies books you want online.
3. Get ten great Dummies Tips™ every week.
4. Chat with your favorite ...For Dummies authors.
5. Subscribe free to The Dummies Dispatch™ newsletter.
6. Enter our sweepstakes and win cool stuff.
7. Send a free cartoon postcard to a friend.
8. Download free software.
9. Sample a book before you buy.
10. Talk to us. Make comments, ask questions, and get answers!

Jump online to these ten fun and useful things at

http://www.dummies.com/10useful

For other technology titles from IDG Books Worldwide, go to
www.idgbooks.com

Not online yet? It's easy to get started with The Internet For Dummies®, 5th Edition, or Dummies 101®: The Internet For Windows® 98, available at local retailers everywhere.

Find other ...*For Dummies* books on these topics:

Business • Careers • Databases • Food & Beverages • Games • Gardening • Graphics
Hardware • Health & Fitness • Internet and the World Wide Web • Networking • Office Suites
Operating Systems • Personal Finance • Pets • Programming • Recreation • Sports
Spreadsheets • Teacher Resources • Test Prep • Word Processing

IDG BOOKS WORLDWIDE BOOK REGISTRATION

Register This Book and Win!

We want to hear from you!

Visit **http://my2cents.dummies.com** to register this book and tell us how you liked it!

- ✔ Get entered in our monthly prize giveaway.

- ✔ Give us feedback about this book — tell us what you like best, what you like least, or maybe what you'd like to ask the author and us to change!

- ✔ Let us know any other *...For Dummies*® topics that interest you.

Your feedback helps us determine what books to publish, tells us what coverage to add as we revise our books, and lets us know whether we're meeting your needs as a *...For Dummies* reader. You're our most valuable resource, and what you have to say is important to us!

Not on the Web yet? It's easy to get started with *Dummies 101*®: *The Internet For Windows*® *98* or *The Internet For Dummies*,® 5th Edition, at local retailers everywhere.

Or let us know what you think by sending us a letter at the following address:

...For Dummies Book Registration
Dummies Press
7260 Shadeland Station, Suite 100
Indianapolis, IN 46256-3945
Fax 317-596-5498

™

BESTSELLING BOOK SERIES FROM IDG